Make Gentle the
Life of This World

June 12, 2015

Dear Graduate,

I have always given a copy of this favorite book of Joe McHale to the person who is chosen by the faculty to get the award in his name. You must be very much like him and so fit the criterion for this award. I look forward to knowing you and ask my Joe to smile down on you and watch over you as you begin a new part of your life. May you continue to do well in your studies, care about others, and be yourself.

All the best to you.
Rose McHale

Make Gentle the Life of This World

THE VISION OF ROBERT F. KENNEDY

Edited and with an Introduction by
MAXWELL TAYLOR KENNEDY

BROADWAY BOOKS
New York

Broadway Books titles may be purchased for business or promotional use or for special sales. For information, please write to: Special Markets Department, Random House, Inc., 1540 Broadway, New York, NY 10036.

BROADWAY BOOKS and its logo, a letter B bisected on the diagonal, are trademarks of Broadway Books, a division of Random House, Inc.

First Broadway Books trade paperback edition published 1999.

Designed by Kaelin Chappell

Library of Congress Cataloging-in-Publication Data

Kennedy, Robert F., 1925–1968.
    Make gentle the life of the world : the vision of Robert F.
F. Kennedy / edited and with an introduction by Maxwell Taylor Kennedy.
      p. cm.
    Includes bibliographical references
    ISBN 0–7679-0371-4 (pb)
    1. Kennedy, Robert F., 1925–1968—Quotations.   2. Conduct of life–Quotations, maxims, etc.   3. Quotations, American.   I. Kennedy,
Maxwell Taylor.   II. Title.
[E840.922'092—dc21   98-55988
                                     CIP

10 9 8 7 6

None can usurp the height but those
to whom the miseries of the world
are a misery and will not let them rest.

—UNKNOWN,
from Robert F. Kennedy's daybook

Contents

Acknowledgments

This book is dedicated to my brother Michael, whose love always shone in his eyes and who made me feel safe wherever we were.

And to my mother, whom Daddy loved most of all and whose love sustained him and enabled him to reach out each day, and to dare.

I wish to acknowledge first and foremost my wife, Vicki, whom my father never knew but whom I know he would have loved deeply. Without her love and sweet intellect, joy, kindness, and friendship over the last eleven years, I would not have had the capacity to pull together this little book. I also want to thank my two little children, who have given me just enough fatherly insight to finish this compilation.

I would like to thank my Uncle Teddy, who took such good care of us after my father was killed and always insured that we would understand what my father had tried to do. Teddy's book, *Words Jack Loved,* moved me considerably when I was little and, really, formed the basis for my work here.

I would like to thank Walt Bode at Harcourt Brace, whose commitment to the idea of this book was unwavering. He was the best editor I could imagine and made me believe that nearly every change was my idea. Doe Coover's early support was essential, and Theo Lieber, who has worked hard on this at Harcourt, was also very supportive. Marianna Lee kept everything in place, Suzanne Cokal and Dan Janeck fixed missteps in the text, and Esin Goknar tracked down the photographers whose photos may not have seen daylight in a generation.

I would especially like to thank Ena Bernard, without whose constant and thoughtful help this book could not have been written. I would also like to thank Dirk and Bill Ziff for their help reading early drafts and David Michaelis and Eleanor Cunningham Carey for their help with the book and the proposal. Lynn Delaney and Andrew Glasso amazed me with their willingness to dig through endless files at Hickory Hill, tracking elusive photos and notes of my father's. Wes Hill and Randolph Bell spent many hours in the John F. Kennedy Library, and many others submerged in Widener Library, searching for documents and photos.

I would like to thank the staff of the John F. Kennedy Library, especially Will Johnson and Meaghan Desnoyers. Allen Goodrich seemed to know the precise location of every photograph ever taken of RFK. Many friends helped me by reading drafts of this book: I would like to thank Bob Rodman, Allen Wheelis, and Bob Coles, whose insights were a most valuable contribution. Thanks, too, to Brando Quilici.

I would like to thank Bonnie and Roger Gould, Ben and Iliana Strauss, and Evan and Stacey Strauss, who have taught me so much about being a family member. A special thanks to Bob Corcoran, Virginia Desario, and Joe Hakim, who worked hard so that I did not have to. Kent Correl, Jeff Sachs, David Lande, Sabrina Padwa, Michael Mailor, Clay Tatum, Mark Bailey, and Joe Driscoll helped very much in the final days when the manuscript was due. Virgilio Barco, Amir Farman-Farmaian, Pedro Mezquita, and John and Noella Jane were also very supportive. Paul Ryan was selfless with his time and skill.

Perhaps the greatest aid in the writing of this book was the work of Edwin O. Guthman and C. Richard Allen, whose book *RFK: Collected Speeches* was my greatest resource and which anyone who likes the present book should immediately read.

I would like to give a special thanks to the speechwriters who helped my father: Peter Edelman, Jeff Greenfield, Ted Sorenson, and especially Adam Walinsky and Richard Goodwin, who have continued to be available to me.

I owe a huge debt to the friends and associates of my father who completed their memoirs or biographies of him. Their books gave me an opportunity to learn more about my father than most fatherless children can ever hope to receive. I am grateful for the work of Jack Newfield, Jules Witcover, David

Halberstam, and, more than anyone, Arthur J. Schlesinger, Jr., whose biography of my father I relied on heavily for this short work. It remains my favorite history.

Finally, I would like to thank my brothers and sisters, Kathleen, Joe, Bobby, Courtney, Kerry, Christopher, Douglas, and Rory, for putting up with yet another Kennedy book.

Introduction

I guess more than anything this book began as a little boy's search for his father. About a year or so ago, my mother asked me to put together a book of quotations from my father's speeches. I avoided the project at first. I had built a life somewhat independent of my family, and I did not want to spend so much time on a project that would be inextricably identified with it. I also felt trepidation at the daunting task of spending so much time thinking about my father.

Finally, I had my own family to care for. I had two little children of my own, and my wife, Vicki, had just begun working again. (She had cared for Maxey and Summer during my years trying cases as an assistant district attorney, and now we had traded places: Vicki was a teaching fellow at Harvard, and I was taking care of our children.)

My son was just reaching the age I was when my father was killed. As I watched my own little boy, I thought more and more about my father, his work, and his life.

In Vicki's literature courses, she is always trying to make the characters in the books she teaches become real for her students, to become companions her students can hold on to as they make their way in the world—guides to help with their various struggles in life. I thought about the many books that have been written about my father, and then about the many stories about him in publications of all sorts; and I thought how few people had read these books. These days, information comes at us so quickly and thickly.

I thought that I would like to try to make Robert F. Kennedy available both to those who remember him and what he tried to do, and to those whose only information about him may have come from television. I wanted to create a book that could tell readers a little of who RFK was, even if they had only a few moments available.

As a son who lost his father early and to violence, I guess this book in some way attempts to put together the various pieces—the letters, the statements, the recordings, the pictures, the thoughts—to render a life. It is a life that is important for me as a son, but also important for me as an American who is looking not merely for a father who is gone, but for leadership, and perhaps even heroism.

My father was of the last generation to grow up in a time when Americans made an effort to remain consistent. Few of his peers thought much about reinventing themselves for some kind of gain; constancy was prized more than material success. We live in more complicated times. My father was an important bridge between two generations, across what was perhaps the greatest "gap" in the history of the country.

Most people become more and more set as they grow older. My father became more flexible, yet his core values and morality remained constant.

Americans seem to have two natures, one extraordinarily positive and forthright, the other dark and cynical. Historically, in challenging times, it has been easiest for politicians to appeal to that baser side. Thus we've had the success of Father Coughlin and Huey Long during the depression, and later, of George Wallace. (It has always struck me as odd that virtually all of the Democrats who supported George Wallace had previously been RFK Democrats. The same Americans who voted for Wallace were able to share RFK's vision of this country—a much different view.) I have never come across a public pronouncement by RFK in which he made an appeal to the darker side.

My father was not a typically introspective person. Few of his personal letters offer much real insight into himself. He seems rather to have been most insightful during moments devoted to other people. Preparing for this book, I began reading books about my father written by people who knew him well. Each time he was quoted, I underlined. I also read through the many letters he wrote home from school, and from the Navy, and from his travels. I read the letters he sent to his friends, and the ones he saved from them. I read from papers he wrote in law school. I reread the letters he wrote to us, his children. I read the private essay he wrote about his own father. I read virtually every speech he ever made. (I found them remarkable documents. I had read them often as I grew up, and I wanted to bring a part of the impact of that language to an audience that perhaps does not have time to read through RFK's collected speeches.) I reread the books he wrote, about mob rackets, about foreign policy, about the Cuban missile crisis.

He wrote mostly about America, where the country was, where he thought we were heading, and where we should be heading. And throughout his work he emphasized our responsibilities as citizens and as human beings, to ourselves and to each other.

Many of his most profound statements about the world, about society, and even about himself come in his public speeches. He had help. There is the unmistakable polish of many speechwriters from the years in Washington. Most significant is the impact of the three young writers: Peter Edelman, Adam Walinsky, and Jeff Greenfield. All under thirty, they contributed much to his words.

Finally I read and reread my father's daybook. It had begun as a joint project with President Kennedy, who kept a book in which he wrote down quotations from his readings that struck him as interesting, or funny, or poignant in some way. When Jack died, my father continued the book and expanded it, using the quotations in many of his speeches. He would quote Aeschylus when he spoke to the poorest audiences that a presidential candidate had ever bothered with, and they cheered.

I read the Greek translations that so moved him. I went through old bookshelves and read his well-thumbed and underlined copy of *The Echo of Greece,* by Edith Hamilton. I found a little box hidden away at our home, Hickory Hill, filled with quotations he had taken from Camus. I went back and I found the old poems and plays, the essays by Camus that he loved. And I read them again.

I have tried to put together here a picture of a man. This book is not about specific policy concerns, though it may bring to mind many of the real challenges of the 1960s, nor is it much of a personal account. This book is not history, neither essay nor biography, and it is not even strictly a book of quotations. It contains not only quotations from Robert F. Kennedy, but also many from other sources cited in his daybook. These are the words he spoke to challenge and inspire us, and also the words he read that inspired and challenged him. The selections in this book can be read almost like poetry, or as meditations for someone who wants to think about Robert Kennedy and the 1960s and the nature of politics and leadership. It is my hope that people will read this book and think back to a time, a generation ago, when the country was much smaller. That they will think a little bit about who we were and what we have become—that the reader who is willing to spend a few hours will find reason to wonder what it means to be a politician, to be an American, and to contribute to one's family, society, and country.

— MAXWELL TAYLOR KENNEDY
October 1997

RFK
1925–1968

Here in my study, in its listlessness
of Vacancy, some old Victorian house,
air-tight and sheeted for old summers,
far from the hornet yatter of the bond—
is loneliness, a thin smoke thread of vital
air. What can I catch from you now?
Doom was woven in your nerves, your shirt,
woven in the great clan; they, too, were loyal,
you, too, were more than loyal to them . . . to death.
For them, like a prince, you daily left your tower
to walk through dirt in your best cloth. Here now,
alone, in my Plutarchan bubble, I miss
you, you out of Plutarch, made by hand—
Forever approaching our maturity.

— ROBERT LOWELL

The Act of Living

You knew that what is given or granted can be taken away, that what is begged can be refused; but that what is earned is kept, that what is self-made is inalienable, that what you do for yourselves and for your children can never be taken away.

As life is action and passion, it is required of a man that he should share the passion and action of his time, at peril of being judged not to have lived.

— OLIVER WENDELL HOLMES

Action is with the scholar subordinate, but it is essential. Without it he is not yet man. Without it thought can never ripen into truth.

— RALPH WALDO EMERSON

It is simple to follow the easy and familiar path of personal ambition and private gain. It is more comfortable to sit content in the easy approval of friends and of neighbors than to risk the friction and the controversy that comes with public affairs. It is easier to fall in step with the slogans of others than to march to the beat of the internal drummer—to make and stand on judgments of your own. And it is far easier to accept and to stand on the past, than to fight for the answers of the future.

There is always room at the top.　　　—DANIEL WEBSTER

A Constant Effort

God offers to everyone his choice between truth and repose. Take which you please—you can never have both.

—RALPH WALDO EMERSON

We all struggle to transcend the cruelties and the follies of mankind. That struggle will not be won by standing aloof and pointing a finger; it will be won by action, by men who commit their every resource of mind and body to the education and improvement and help of their fellow man.

[from a memoir of Joseph P. Kennedy, Sr.]
He has called on the best that was in us. There was no such thing as half-trying. Whether it was running a race or catching a football, competing in school—we were to try. And we were to try harder than anyone else. We might not be the best, and none of us were, but we were to make the effort to be the best. "After you have done the best you can," he used to say, "the hell with it."

He only earns his freedom and existence who daily conquers them anew.　　　　　　　　　　　　　　　　　　—GOETHE

[During one of RFK's speeches, a student in the crowd asked, "Where are you going to get all the money for these federally subsidized programs you're talking about?"]
From you. Let me say something about the tenor of that question and some of the other questions. There are people in this country who suffer. I look around this room and I don't see many black faces who are going to be doctors. You can talk about where the money will come from. . . . Part of civilized society is to let people go to medical school who come from ghettos. You don't see many people coming out of the ghettos or off the Indian reservations to medical school. You are the privileged ones here. It's easy to sit back and say it's the fault of the federal

government, but it's our responsibility, too. It's our society, not just our government, that spends twice as much on pets as on the poverty program. It's the poor who carry the major burden of the struggle in Vietnam. You sit here as white medical students while black people carry the burden of the fighting in Vietnam.

The great French marshal [Louis-Hubert-Gonzalve] Lyautey once asked his gardener to plant a tree. The gardener objected that the tree was slow growing and would not reach maturity for one hundred years. The marshal replied, "In that case, there's no time to lose. Plant it this afternoon."

These were a decent people. Their only monument: the asphalt road and a thousand lost golf balls.   —T. S. ELIOT
[RFK added] I think we can do better than that.

We are on them not to see if the lines are straight but to play tennis.   —ROBERT FROST

It is not enough to understand, or to see clearly. The future will be shaped in the arena of human activity, by those willing to commit their minds and their bodies to the task.

The hottest places in Hell are reserved for those who in time of moral crisis preserve their neutrality.   DANTE

In this theater of man's life, it is reserved only for God and for angels to be lookers on.   — FRANCIS BACON

I think that the picture in the paper of a child drowning should trouble us more than it does, or the picture last week of a paratrooper holding a rifle to a woman's head, it must trouble us more than it does.

A journey of a thousand miles must begin with a single step.

— LAO-TZU

An American Spirit

AMERICA

All of us, from the wealthiest to the young children that I have seen in this country, in this year, bloated by starvation—we all share one precious possession, and that is the name *American*.

It is not easy to know what that means.

But in part to be an American means to have been an outcast and a stranger, to have come to the exiles' country, and to know that he who denies the outcast and stranger still amongst us, he also denies America.

History has placed us all, Northerner and Southerner, black and white, within a common border and under a common law. All of us, from the wealthiest and most powerful of men, to the weakest and hungriest of children, share one precious possession: the name *American*.   —JOHN F. KENNEDY

We steer our ship with hope, leaving Fear astern.

— THOMAS JEFFERSON

The essence of the American Revolution—the principle on which this country was founded—is that direct participation in political activity is what makes a free society.

A Continuing Evolution

"We must consider that we shall be as a city, set upon a hill, and the eyes of all people will be upon us."

The Puritans were in the middle of the Atlantic when they shared that vision of the city upon the hill. We are still in the middle of our journey. As long as millions of Americans suffer indignity, and punishment, and deprivation because of their color, their poverty, and our inaction, we know that we are only halfway to our goal—only halfway to a city upon a hill, a city in which we can all take pride, a city and a country in which the promises of our Constitution are at last fulfilled for all Americans.

Think how our world would look to a visitor from another planet as he crossed the continents. He would find great cities and knowledge able to create enormous abundance from the materials of nature. He would witness exploration into understanding of the entire physical universe, from the particles of the atom to the secrets of life. He would see billions of people separated by only a few hours of flight, communicating with the speed of light, sharing a common dependence on a thin layer of soil and a covering of air. Yet he would also observe that most of mankind was living in misery and hunger, that some of the inhabitants of this tiny, crowded globe were killing others, and that a few patches of land were pointing huge instruments of death and war at others. Since what he was seeing proved our intelligence, he would only wonder at our sanity.

It is this monstrous absurdity—that in the midst of such possibility, men should hate and kill and oppress one another—that must be the target of the modern American revolution. ⌒

On this generation of Americans falls the full burden of proving to the world that we really mean it when we say all men are created free and are equal before the law. All of us might wish at times that we lived in a more tranquil world, but we don't. And if our times are difficult and perplexing, so are they challenging and filled with opportunity.

But all our great cooperative efforts will come to little if they do not succeed in restoring importance to the lives of individual men. Long ago the Greeks defined happiness as "the exercise of vital powers along lines of excellence in a life affording them scope." The fulfillment of that objective is increasingly difficult in the face of the giant organizations and massive bureaucracies of the age. Still it is what we must seek, helping men and communities to mark off a corner of the world in which to move, to stretch mind and body in the effort "not only to equal or resemble, but to excel," which John Adams told us would forever be "the great spring of human action"—and which was our goal for ourselves and one another in our compact two short centuries ago.

Each of our cities is now the seat of nearly all the problems of American life: poverty and race hatred, interrupted education and stunted lives, and the other ills of the new urban nation—

congestion and the filth, danger, and purposelessness, which afflict all but the very rich and the very lucky. To speak of the urban conditions, therefore, is to speak of the condition of American life.

Not a decade has gone by in our nation's history in which we did not undergo new experiences and seek new challenges. We were born in a revolution against colonialism, and we have been dedicated ever since to revolution for freedom and progress.

The American Journey has not ended. America is never accomplished. America is always still to build; for men, as long as they are truly men, will dream of man's fulfillment.

— ARCHIBALD MACLEISH

America was a great force in the world, with immense prestige, long before we became a great military power. That power has come to us and we cannot renounce it, but neither can we afford to forget that the real constructive force in the world comes not from bombs but from imaginative ideas, warm sympathies, and a generous spirit.

Over the years, an understanding of what America really stands for is going to count far more than missiles, aircraft carriers, and supersonic bombers.

John Adams once said that he considered the founding of America part of "a divine plan for the liberation of the slavish part of mankind all over the globe."

This faith did not spring from grandiose schemes of empires abroad.

It grew instead from confidence that the example set by our nation—the example of individual liberty fused with common effort—would spark the spirit of liberty around the planet; and that once unleashed, no despot could suppress it, no prison could restrain it, no army could withstand it.

A Moral Vision

Dangerous changes in American life are indicated by what is going on in America today. Disaster is our destiny unless we reinstall the toughness, the moral idealism which has guided this nation during its history. The paramount interest in oneself, for money, for material goods, for security, must be replaced by an interest in one another—an actual, not just a vocal, interest in our country; a search for adventure, a willingness to fight, and a will to win; a desire to serve our community, our schools, our nation.

So if we are uneasy about our country today, perhaps it is because we are truer to our principles than we realize, because we know that our happiness will come not from goods we have but from the good we do together. . . .

We say with Camus: "I should like to be able to love my country and still love justice."

Debate and dissent are the very heart of the American process. We have followed the wisdom of Greece: "All things are to be examined and brought into question. There is no limit set to thought."

Our ideal of America is a nation in which justice is done; and therefore, the continued existence of injustice—of unnecessary, inexcusable poverty in this most favored of nations—this knowledge erodes our ideal of America, our basic sense of who and what we are. It is, in the deepest sense of the word, demoralizing—to all of us.

I love my country too much to be a nationalist.

—ALBERT CAMUS

We must dare to remember what President Kennedy said we could not dare to forget—that we are the heirs of a revolution that lit the imagination of all those who seek a better life for themselves and their children.

As long as men are hungry, and their children uneducated, and their crops destroyed by pestilence, the American Revolution will have a part to play. As long as men are not free—in their lives and their opinions, their speech and their knowledge—that long will the American Revolution not be finished.

With some trepidation, I argued [during the Cuban Missile Crisis] that, whatever validity the military and political arguments were for an attack in preference to a blockade, America's traditions and history would not permit such a course of action. Whatever military reasons he and others could marshal, they were nevertheless, in the last analysis, advocating a surprise attack by a very large nation against a very small one. This, I said, could not be undertaken by the U.S. if we were to maintain our moral position at home and around the globe. Our struggle against Communism throughout the world was for far more than physical survival—it had as its essence our heritage and our ideals, and these we must not destroy.

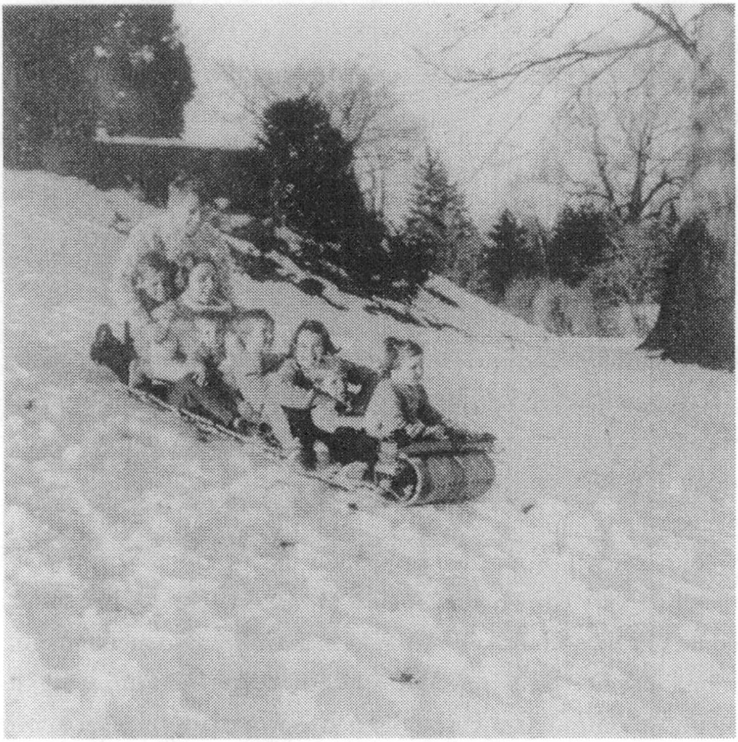

Our gross national product, now, is over eight hundred billion dollars a year, but that GNP—if we should judge America by that—counts air pollution and cigarette advertising, and ambulances to clear our highways of carnage. It counts special locks for our doors and the jails for those who break them. It counts the destruction of our redwoods and the loss of our natural wonder in chaotic sprawl. It counts napalm and the cost of a nuclear warhead, and armored cars for police who fight riots in our streets. It counts Whitman's rifle and Speck's knife, and the television programs which glorify violence in order to sell toys to our children.

Yet the gross national product does not allow for the health of our children, the quality of their education, or the joy of their play. It does not include the beauty of our poetry or the strength of our marriages, the intelligence of our public debate or the integrity of our public officials. It measures neither our wit nor our courage, neither our wisdom nor our learning, neither our compassion nor our devotion to our country; it measures everything, in short, except that which makes life worthwhile. And it can tell us everything about America except why we are proud that we are Americans. ~

The Bonds Between Us

Jefferson Davis once came to Boston, and he addressed his audience in Faneuil Hall as "countrymen, brethren, Democrats." Rivers of blood and years of darkness divide that day from this. But those words echo down to this hall, bringing the lesson that only as countrymen and as brothers can we hope to master and subdue to the service of mankind the enormous forces which rage across the world in which all of us live. And only in this way can we pursue our personal talents to the limits of our possibility—not as Northerners or Southerners, blacks or whites, but as men and women in the service of the American dream.

But one thing at least unites all of us—and that is our love of our common soil, and our anguish. Anguish as we face a future that closes up a little every day, as we face the threat of a degrading struggle, of an economic disequilibrium that is already serious and is increasing every day, that may reach the point where no effort will be able to revive Algeria for a long time to come.

—ALBERT CAMUS

FREEDOM

No citizen can escape from freedom and still enjoy it.

He only earns his freedom and existence who daily conquers them anew. — GOETHE

We know that if one man's rights are denied, the rights of all are endangered.

Freedom means not only the opportunity to know but the will to know.

Thomas Paine once said that "no man or country can be really free unless all men and all countries are free."

Freedom is not money, that I could enlarge mine by taking yours. Our liberty can grow only when the liberties of all our fellow men are secure; and he who would enslave others ends only by chaining himself, for chains have two ends, and he who holds the chain is as securely bound as he whom it holds. And as President Kennedy said at the Berlin Wall in 1963, "Freedom is indivisible, and when one man is enslaved, all are not free."

The contention was that we needed justice first and that we would come to freedom later on, as if slaves could ever hope to achieve justice. And forceful intellectuals announced to the worker that bread alone interested him rather than freedom, as if the worker didn't know that his bread depends in part on his freedom.   — ALBERT CAMUS

DEMOCRACY

Everything that makes man's life worthwhile—family, work, education, a place to rear one's children, and a place to rest one's head—all this depends on decisions of government; all can be swept away by a government which does not heed the demands of its people. Therefore, the essential humanity of men can be protected and preserved only where government must answer—not just to the wealthy, not just to those of a particular religion, or a particular race, but to all its people.

A tyrant disturbs ancient laws, violates women, kills men without trial. But a people ruling—first, the very name of it is so beautiful; and secondly; a people does none of these things.

— HERODOTUS

There is no despot in our land, no man
Who rules and makes laws at his own desire.
Free is our city, here the people rule,
rich man and poor held equal by the law.

— EURIPIDES

I believe in democracy, because it releases the energy of every
human being. — WOODROW WILSON

There are hazards in debating American policy in the face of a
stern and dangerous enemy. But that hazard is the essence of
our democracy. Democracy is no easy form of government. Few
nations have been able to sustain it. For it requires that we take
the chances of freedom; that the liberating play of reason be
brought to bear on events filled with passion; that dissent be al-
lowed to make its appeal for acceptance; that men chance error
in their search for the truth. . . .

DEBATE AND DISSENT

The future does not belong to those who are content with today, apathetic toward common problems and their fellow man alike, timid and fearful in the face of new ideas and bold projects. Rather it will belong to those who can blend passion, reason, and courage in a personal commitment to the ideals and great enterprises of American society. It will belong to those who see that wisdom can only emerge from the clash of contending views, the passionate expression of deep and hostile beliefs. Plato said: "A life without criticism is not worth living."

For it is not enough to allow dissent. We must demand it. For there is much to dissent from.

This is what separated us from you; we made demands. You were satisfied to serve the power of your nation and we dreamed of giving ours her truth.　　　—ALBERT CAMUS

The Constitution protects wisdom and ignorance, compassion and selfishness alike. But that dissent which consists simply of sporadic and dramatic acts sustained by neither continuing labor or research—that dissent which seeks to demolish while lacking both the desire and direction for rebuilding, that dissent which, contemptuously or out of laziness, casts aside the practical weapons and instruments of change and progress—that kind of dissent is merely self-indulgence. It is satisfying, perhaps, only to those who make it.

If our colleges and universities do not breed men who riot, who rebel, who attack life with all the youthful vision and vigor, then there is something wrong with our colleges. The more riots that come on college campuses, the better world for tomorrow.

　　　　　　　　　　　—WILLIAM ALLEN WHITE

The Basis of Democracy

Every dictatorship has ultimately strangled in the web of repression it wove for its people, making mistakes that could not be corrected because criticism was prohibited.

There are millions of Americans living in hidden places, whose faces and names we never know. But I have seen children starving in Mississippi, idling their lives away in the ghetto, living without hope or future amid the despair on Indian reservations, with no jobs and little hope. I have seen proud men in the hills of Appalachia, who wish only to work in dignity—but the mines are closed, and the jobs are gone, and no one, neither industry or labor or government, has cared enough to help. Those conditions will change, those children will live, only if we dissent. So I dissent, and I know you do, too.

*Seeking a
Better World*

CIVIL RIGHTS

We must recognize the full human equality of all of our people—before God, before the law, and in the councils of government. We must do this, not because it is economically advantageous, although it is; not because of the laws of God command it, although they do; not because people in other lands wish it so. We must do it for the single and fundamental reason that it is the right thing to do.

A Different Perspective

But if any man claims the Negro should be content or satisfied, let him say he would willingly change the color of his skin and go to live in the Negro section of a large city. Then, and only then, has he a right to such a claim.

They see us spend billions on armaments while poverty and ignorance continue at home; they see us willing to fight a war for freedom in Vietnam, but unwilling to fight with one-hundredth the money or force or effort to secure freedom in Mississippi or Alabama or the ghettos of the North.

Suppose God Is Black.

Two Worlds

We live in different worlds and gaze out over a different landscape. Through our eyes in the white majority, the Negro world is one of steady and continuous progress. In a few years, he has seen the entire discriminatory legislation torn down. He has heard Presidents become spokesmen for racial justice, while black Americans enter the cabinet and the Supreme Court.

The white American has paid taxes for poverty and education programs, and watched his children risk their lives to register voters in Alabama. Seeing this, he asks, what cause can there be for violent insurrection, of dissatisfaction with present progress? But if we try to look through the eyes of the young slum-dweller—the Negro, and the Puerto Rican, and the Mexican American—the world is a dark and hopeless place indeed.

Let us look for a moment. The chances are that he was born into a family without a father, often as a result of welfare laws which require a broken home as a condition for help. I have seen, in my own state of New York, these children crowded with adults into one or two rooms, without adequate plumbing or heat, each night trying to defend against marauding rats. The growing child goes to a school which teaches little that helps him in an alien world. The chances are seven of ten that he will not graduate from high school; and even when he does, he has a fifty-fifty chance of acquiring only as much as the equivalent of an eighth grade education. A young college graduate who taught in a ghetto school sums it up this way: "The books are junk, the paint peels, the cellar stinks, the teachers call you nigger, the windows fall in on your head."

But this is not all the young man of the ghetto can see. Every day, as the years pass, and he becomes aware that there is nothing at the end of the road, he watches the rest of us go from peak to new peak of comfort. A few blocks away or in his television set, the young Negro of the slums sees the multiplying marvels of white America: more new cars and more summer vacations, more air-conditioned homes and neatly kept lawns. But he cannot buy them.

He is told that Negroes are making progress. But what can that mean to him? He cannot experience the progress of others, nor should we seriously expect him to feel grateful because he is no longer a slave, or because he can vote, or eat at some lunch counters. He sees only the misery of his present and of the darkening years ahead. Others tell him to work his way up as other minorities have done; and so he must. For he knows and we know that only by his own efforts and his own labor will the Negro come to full equality.

A Deeper Commitment

In the last five or six years, the white people have looked at the black people and said, "Look at all we have done. We passed the Civil Rights Act of 1964. We passed the Civil Rights Act of 1965. A Negro has been appointed to the Supreme Court. A Negro has been appointed to the cabinet. We passed the poverty program. We've done all of these things. And we spent all of this money; and yet there are riots in the cities. And there's lawlessness. And there's violence. And there's looting. Don't the black people understand what we've tried to do and that we've made this commitment and can't they be satisfied?"

The black person, on the other hand, says, "That's all fine for Mr. Weaver, who's in the cabinet. And that's fine for Mr. Marshall, who's on the Supreme Court. And that's fine for the civil rights bills that have been passed. But none of that has any effect on my life. The fact is my children still go to substandard schools. The fact is my husband can't get a job. The fact is that I can't get welfare unless I divorce my husband and my children are illegitimate."

The fact is that the housing is substandard and becoming more substandard. And the fact is, as the Kerner Commission and the Riot Commission reported, the conditions in the ghetto and the conditions for the poor are getting worse, not better.

So that just to have the black people understand the fact that white people want to do what is right and feel that they have taken steps may not be sufficient. But basically there is this [need] for generosity and compassion, to have the white people understand that the conditions are still very difficult for black people.

But as we are learning now, it is one thing to assure a man the legal right to eat in a restaurant; it is another thing to assure that he can earn the money to eat there.

It is a shocking fact—but it is a fact nonetheless—that . . . our . . . whole array of government computers, which threaten to compile on some reel of tape every bit of information ever recorded on the people in this room—this system nowhere records the names or faces or identities of a million Negro men.

schools.... to date is my presumption. I get tired, I get tired, tired.... I will not intend to leave my land-strong children to other whites.

...in a lake next to it was... in his neighbors... while and of our... most... context... to that this way...

we express... such of... boy were... whiter are...

improve our she 10 to sh... on... the more... before

and in these... is...

The federal government has no moral choice but to take the initiative. How can we say to a Negro in Jackson, "When a war comes you will be an American citizen, but in the meantime you're a citizen of Mississippi and we can't help you?"

We have demanded that he obey the same laws as white men, pay the same taxes, fight and die in the same wars. Yet in nearly every part of the country, he remains the victim of humiliation and deprivation no white citizen would tolerate. All thinking Americans have grown increasingly aware that discrimination must stop—not only because it is legally insupportable, economically wasteful, and socially destructive, but above all because it is morally wrong. . . .

White people of whatever kind—even prostitutes, narcotics pushers, Communists, or bank robbers—are welcome at establishments which will not admit certain of our federal judges, ambassadors, and countless members of our Armed Forces. . . . If Congress can, and does, control the service of oleomargarine in every restaurant in the nation, surely it can ensure our nonwhite citizens access to those restaurants. ⌒⌒

ON THE DEATH OF THE REVEREND
DR. MARTIN LUTHER KING, JR.

I have bad news for you, for all of our fellow citizens, and for people who love peace all over the world, and that is that Martin Luther King was shot and killed tonight.

Martin Luther King dedicated his life to love and to justice for his fellow human beings, and he died because of that effort.

In this difficult day, in this difficult time for the United States, it is perhaps well to ask what kind of a nation we are and what direction we want to move in. For those of you who are black—considering the evidence there evidently is that there were white people who were responsible—you can be filled with bitterness, with hatred, and with a desire for revenge. We can move in that direction as a country, in great polarization—black people amongst black, white people amongst white, filled with hatred toward one another.

Or we can make an effort, as Martin Luther King did, to understand and to comprehend, and to replace that violence, that stain of bloodshed that has spread across our land, with an effort to understand with compassion and love.

For those of you who are black and are tempted to be filled with hatred and distrust at the injustice of such an act, against all white people, I can only say that I feel in my own heart the same kind of feeling. I had a member of my family killed, but he was killed by a white man. But we have to make an effort in the United States, we have to make an effort to understand, to go beyond these rather difficult times.

My favorite poet was Aeschylus. He wrote: "In our sleep, pain which cannot forget falls drop by drop upon the heart until, in our own despair, against our will, comes wisdom through the awful grace of God."

What we need in the United States is not division; what we need in the United States is not hatred; what we need in the United States is not violence or lawlessness; but love and wisdom, and compassion toward one another, and a feeling of justice toward those who still suffer within our country, whether they be white or they be black.

So I shall ask you tonight to return home—to say a prayer for the family of Martin Luther King, that's true, but more importantly to say a prayer for our own country, which all of us love—a prayer for understanding and that compassion of which I spoke.

We can do well in this country. We will have difficult times; we've had difficult times in the past; we will have difficult times in the future. It is not the end of violence; it is not the end of lawlessness; it is not the end of disorder.

But the vast majority of white people and the vast majority of black people in this country want to live together, want to improve the quality of our life, and want justice for all human beings who abide in our land.

Let us dedicate ourselves to what the Greeks wrote so many years ago: to tame the savageness of man and make gentle the life of this world.

Let us dedicate ourselves to that, and say a prayer for our country and for our people. ⌒‿

Among Negro youth we can sense, in their alienation, a frustration so terrible, an energy and determination so great, that it must find constructive outlet or result in unknowable danger for us all. This alienation will be reduced to reasonable proportions, in the end, only by bringing the Negro into his rightful place in this nation. But we must work to try and understand, to speak and touch across the gap, and not leave their voices of protest to echo unheard in the ghetto of our ignorance.

The brutalities of Selma, and its denial of elementary rights of citizenship, were condemned throughout the North; and thousands of white Northerners went there to march to Montgomery.

But the many brutalities of the North receive no such attention. I have been in tenements in Harlem in the past several weeks where the smell of rats was so strong that it was difficult to stay there for five minutes, and where children slept with lights turned on their feet to discourage attacks. . . .

Thousands do not flock to Harlem to protest these conditions—much less to change them.

To understand is not to permit. But to fail to understand is the surest guarantee of a mounting strife which will assault the well-being of every citizen. And therefore . . . the first task before us is this: an effort to understand. For the division between black and white is not a failure of compassion, or of the American sense of justice. It is a failure of communication and vision.

CRIME AND VIOLENCE

[The day after Martin Luther King died RFK gave this speech:]
This is a time of shame and sorrow. It is not a day for politics.
I have saved this one opportunity, my only event of today, to
speak briefly to you about the mindless menace of violence in
America which again stains our land and every one of our
lives.

It is not the concern of any one race. The victims of the violence are black and white, rich and poor, young and old, famous
and unknown. They are, most important of all, human beings
whom other human beings loved and needed. No one—no
matter where he lives or what he does—can be certain who will
suffer from some senseless act of bloodshed. And yet it goes on
and on and on in this country of ours.

Why? What has violence ever accomplished? What has it
ever created? No martyr's cause has ever been stilled by his as-
sassin's bullet.

No wrongs have ever been righted by riots and civil disorders. A sniper is only a coward, not a hero; and an uncontrolled, uncontrollable mob is only the voice of madness, not the voice of reason.

Whenever any American's life is taken by another American unnecessarily—whether it is done in the name of the law or in the defiance of the law, by one man or a gang, in cold blood or in passion, in an attack of violence or in response to violence—whenever we tear at the fabric of the life which another man has painfully and clumsily woven for himself and his children, the whole nation is degraded.

The real threat of crime is what it does to ourselves and our communities. No nation hiding behind locked doors is free, for it is imprisoned by its own fear. No nation whose citizens fear to walk their own streets is healthy, for in isolation lies the poisoning of public participation. A nation which surrenders to crime —whether by indifference or by heavy-handed repression—is a society which has resigned itself to failure. Yet, disturbingly, many Americans seem to regard crime as a pervasive enemy that cannot be defeated.

Thus, the fight against crime is in the last analysis the same as the fight for equal opportunity, or the battle against hunger and deprivation, or the struggle to prevent the pollution of our air and water. It is a fight to preserve that quality of community which is at the root of our greatness; a fight to preserve confidence in ourselves and our fellow citizens; a battle for the quality of our lives.

We know now that the color of an executioner's robe matters little. And we know in our hearts, even through times of passion and discontent, that to add to the quantity of violence in this country is to burden our own lives and mortgage our children's souls, and the best possibilities of the American future.

We have a responsibility to the victims of crime and violence. It is a responsibility to think not only of our own convenience but of the tragedy of sudden death. It is a responsibility to put away childish things, to make the possession and use of firearms a matter undertaken only by serious people who will use them with the restraint and maturity that their dangerous nature deserves—and demands.

Some look for scapegoats, others look for conspiracies, but this much is clear: Violence breeds violence, repression brings retaliation, and only a cleansing of our whole society can remove this sickness from our soul.

Ninety percent of the major racketeers would be out of business by the end of this year if the ordinary citizen, the businessman, the union official, and the public authority stood up to be counted and refused to be corrupted.

Among free men, there can be no successful appeal from the ballot to the bullet; and those who take such appeal are sure to lose their cause and pay the costs.   — ABRAHAM LINCOLN

If there is anything that we've learned during the 1960s, all of us who are here, it is that violence is not the answer to our problems.

And let no one say that violence is the courageous way, that violence is the short route, that violence is the easy route. Because violence will bring no answer: It will bring no answer to your union; it will bring no answer to your people; it will bring no answer to us here in the United States, as a people.

Punishment is not prevention. History offers cold comfort to those who think grievance and despair can be subdued by force. To understand is not to permit; but to fail to understand is the surest guarantee of failure.

But no good is done to men by killing their friends, as I know only too well by now. — ALBERT CAMUS

QUALITY OF LIFE

Even as the drive toward bigness [and] concentration . . . has reached heights never before dreamt of in the past, we have come suddenly to realize how heavy a price we have paid: in overcrowding and pollution of the atmosphere, and impersonality; in growth of organizations, particularly government, so large and powerful that individual effort and importance seem lost; and in loss of the values of nature and community and local diversity that found their nurture in the smaller towns and rural areas of America. And we can see, as we enter the last third of the twentieth century, that the price has been too high.

The question now assumes even greater urgency, as the growth of cities propels us toward the "mass society"—that frightening vision of people as interchangeable units, the middle class as powerless as the poor to affect the decisions of government.

One great problem is sheer growth—growth which crowds people into slums, thrusts suburbs out over the countryside, burdens to the breaking point all our old ways of thought and action, our systems of transport and water supply and education, and our means of raising money to finance these vital services.

A second is destruction of the physical environment, stripping people of contact with sun and fresh air, clean rivers, grass, and trees—condemning them to a life among stone and concrete, neon lights and an endless flow of automobiles. This happens not only in the central city, but in the very suburbs where people once fled to find nature. . . .

A third is the increasing difficulty of transportation, adding concealed, unpaid hours to the workweek; removing men from the social and cultural amenities that are the heart of the city; sending destructive swarms of automobiles across the city, leaving behind them a band of concrete and a poisoned atmosphere. . . .

A fourth destructive force is the concentrated poverty and racial tension of the urban ghetto, a problem so vast that the barest recital of its symptoms is profoundly shocking. . . .

Fifth is both cause and consequence of all the rest. It is the destruction of the sense, and often the fact, of community, of human dialogue, the thousand invisible strands of common experience and purpose, affection and respect, which tie men to their fellows. It is expressed in such words as *community, neighborhood, civic pride, friendship*. It provides the life-sustaining force of human warmth, of security among others, and a sense of one's own human significance in the accepted associations and companionship of others.

Change is crowding our people into cities scarred by slums—encircled by suburbs which sprawl recklessly across the countryside, where movement is difficult, beauty rare, life itself more impersonal, and security imperiled by the lawless.

Therefore, the time has come . . . when we must actively fight bigness and overconcentration, and seek instead to bring the engines of government, of technology, of the economy, fully under the control of our citizens, to recapture and reinforce the values of a more human time and place.

Growth has polluted our water and poisoned our air, and stripped us of contact with sunlight, trees, and lakes. Government has foundered as new agencies have proliferated, splitting tasks and energies among dozens of distant and unconnected bureaus. Individuals have lost touch with the institutions of society, even with one another; and thus have become more and more both perpetrators and victims of coldness, cruelty, and violence.

EMPLOYMENT

We must turn the power and resources of our private enterprise system to the underdeveloped nation within our midst.

This should be done by bringing into the ghettos themselves productive and profitable private industry—creating dignified jobs, not welfare handouts, for the men and youth who now languish in idleness.

We have dealt with female-headed families not by putting the men to work but by giving the mothers and children welfare. They might have wanted fathers and husbands; we have given them checks.

The jobs have fled to the suburbs, or have been replaced by machines, or have moved beyond the reach of those with limited education and skills. . . .

The fact is, if we want to change these conditions—those of us here in this room, those of us who are in the establishment, whether it be business, or labor, or government—we must act.

The fact is that we can act. And the fact is also that we are not acting.

In my judgment, the lack of private enterprise participation is the principal cause of our failure to solve the problem of employment in urban poverty areas.

For example, there was in the entire area of Watts at the time of the riots in 1965 not one movie theater.

Clearly, the most important problem in Harlem is education of every kind. Fathers must learn job skills, and mothers how to buy food economically; students must learn to read, and little children how to speak; and teachers must learn how to teach, and employers how to hire.

The Decency of Work

But the root problem is in the fact of dependency and useless-
ness itself. Unemployment means having nothing to do—
which means nothing to do with the rest of us. To be without
work, to be without use to one's fellow citizens, is to be in truth
the Invisible Man of whom Ralph Ellison wrote.

The answer to the welfare crisis is work, jobs, self-sufficiency,
and family integrity; not a massive new extension of welfare;
not a great new outpouring of guidance counselors to give the
poor more advice. We need jobs, dignified employment at decent pay; the kind of employment that lets a man say to his
community, to his family, to his country, and most important, to
himself, "I helped to build this country. I am a participant in its
great public ventures. I am a man."

Our society—all our values, our views of each other, and our
own self-esteem; the contribution we can make to ourselves,
our families, and the community around us—all these things
are built on the work we do. But too many of the inhabitants of
these areas are without the purpose, the satisfaction, or the dignity that we find in our work.

*[RFK visited a mine in Chile where nearly all the workers were
Communists. The U.S. embassy had specifically kept the mine off his
schedule, and local mine officials begged him not to go down the*

shaft, but he did anyway. The mineshaft went down approximately a mile out under the ocean floor. RFK ventured all the way to the end of the shaft and the workers were ecstatic to see him. When he finally emerged from the mine, RFK remarked to a companion:] "If I worked in this mine, I'd be a Communist, too."

Look through the eyes of the young slum-dweller—the Negro, the Puerto Rican, the Mexican American—at the dark and hopeless world he sees. . . .

On his television set, the young man can still watch the multiplying marvels of white America; the commercials still tell him life is impossible without the latest products of our consumer society.

All this goes on.

But he still cannot buy them.

How overwhelming must be the frustration of this young man—this young American—who, desperately wanting to believe and half believing, finds himself still locked in the slums, his education second rate, unable to get a job, confronted by the open prejudice and subtle hostilities of a white world, and powerless to change his condition or even have an effect on his future.

Others still tell him to work his way up as other minorities have done; and so he must.

For he knows, and we know, that only by his own efforts and his own labor will he come to full equality.

But how is he to work?

POVERTY

Action in adequate measure can wait no longer. There are children in the United States of America with bloated bellies and sores of disease on their bodies. They have cuts and bruises that will not heal correctly in a timely fashion, and chronically runny noses. There are children in the United States who eat so little that they fall asleep in school and do not learn. We must act, and we must act now.

For there is another kind of violence, slower but just as deadly destructive as the shot or the bomb in the night. This is the violence of institutions: indifference and inaction and slow decay. This is the violence that afflicts the poor, that poisons relations between men because their skins have different colors. This is the slow destruction of a child by hunger, and schools without books and homes without heat in the winter.

This is the breaking of a man's spirit by denying him the chance to stand as a father and as a man among other men. And this, too, afflicts us all.

"Well, what joy is there in day that follows day, some swift, some slow, with death the only goal?" Really, that's what many of our fellow citizens feel—whether they're in Appalachia or whether they're in Harlem or whether they're the white children who live in some of these other areas where they've no future.

Dignity and Despair

The poor man's conscience is clear; yet he is ashamed. . . . He feels himself out of the sight of others, groping in the dark. Mankind takes no notice of him. He rambles and wanders unheeded. In the midst of a crowd, at church, in the market . . . he is in as much obscurity as he would be in a garret or a cellar. He is not disapproved, censured, or reproached; he is only not seen. . . . To be wholly overlooked, and to know it, is intolerable. If Crusoe on his island had the library of Alexandria, and a certainty that he should never again see the face of man, would he ever open a volume? — JOHN ADAMS

Our housing projects were built largely without either reference or relevance to the underlying problems of poverty, unemployment, social disorganization, and alienation which caused people to need assistance in the first place. Too many of the projects, as a result, become jungles—places of despair and danger for their residents, and for the cities they were designed to save.

Let [television] show the sound, the feel, the hopelessness, and what it's like to think you'll never get out. Show a black teenager, told by some radio jingle to stay in school, looking at his older brother, who stayed in school, and who's out of a job. Show the Mafia pushing narcotics; put a *Candid Camera* team in a ghetto school and watch what a rotten system of education it really is. Film a mother staying up all night to keep the rats from her baby. . . . Then I'd ask people to watch it and experience what it means to live in the most affluent society in history—without hope.

There are others from whom we avert our sight. Some of them are in the hills and hollows of [the] Appalachians. That is proud land and these are proud men, who have rallied to the nation's flag at every hour of danger. But the deep mines are closing, and the jobs have gone, leaving men without work, many of them crippled by the accidents and disease that lurk "down in the mines," their land a ruin of strip mines and stinking creeks. Their children are ravaged by worms and intestinal parasites. They eat bread and gravy and sometimes beans; and as one of them says, when another child is born "we just add a little water to the gravy."

And there are others: on the back roads of Mississippi, where thousands of children slowly starve their lives away, their minds damaged beyond repair by the age of four or five; in the camps of the migrant workers, a half million nomads virtually unprotected by collective bargaining or social security, minimum wage or workmen's compensation, exposed to the caprice of fate and the cruelty of their fellow man alike; and on Indian reservations where the unemployment rate is 80 percent, and where suicide is not a philosopher's question but the leading cause of death among young people. ⌒

WELFARE

We often quote Lincoln's warning that America could not survive half slave and half free. Nor can it survive while millions of our people are slaves to dependency and poverty, waiting on the favor of their fellow citizens who write them checks. Fellowship, community, shared patriotism—these essential values of our civilization do not come from just buying and consuming goods together. They come from a shared sense of individual independence and personal effort.

They come from working together to build a country—that is the answer to the welfare crisis.

And the effects of the shortage of meaningful employment are reinforced by a welfare structure which is frequently destructive both of individuals and of the community in which they live.

More basically, welfare itself has done much to divide our people, to alienate us one from the other. Partly this separation comes from the understandable resentment of the taxpayer, helplessly watching your welfare rolls and your property tax rise. But there is greater resentment among the poor, the recipients of our charity. Some of it comes from the brutality of the welfare system itself: from the prying bureaucrat, an all-powerful administrator deciding at his desk who is deserving and who is not, who shall live another month and who may starve next week.

Dividing a Nation

If we cannot feed the children of our nation, there is very little we will be able to succeed in doing to live up to the principles which our founders set out nearly two hundred years ago.

So there is our problem. Among us are millions who wish to be part of this society—to share its abundance, its opportunity, and its purposes. We can deny this wish or work to make it come true. If we choose denial then we choose spreading conflict, which will surely erode the well-being and liberty of every citizen and, in a profound way, diminish the idea of America. If we choose fulfillment it will take work but we will choose to improve the well-being of all our people; choose to end fear and heal wounds; and we will choose peace—the only peace that can last—peace with justice.

But of all our problems, the most immediate and pressing, the one that threatens to paralyze our capacity to act, to obliterate our vision of the future, is the plight of the people of the ghetto, and the violence that has exploded as its product—jumping and spreading across the country, sending fear and anger before it, leaving death and devastation behind. We are now, as we may well be for some time to come, in the midst of what is rapidly becoming the most terrible and urgent domestic crisis to face this nation since the Civil War. Its consequences reach into every home, bringing the sure knowledge that failure to deal with this problem could mean failure in dealing with all the other elements of our urban crisis.

The oppressed want to be liberated not only from their hunger but also from their masters. They are well aware that they will be effectively freed of hunger only when they hold their masters, all their masters, at bay.   —ALBERT CAMUS

We learn, at the last, to look at our brothers as aliens, men with whom we share a city, but not a community; men bound to us in common dwelling, but not in common effort. We learn to share only a common fear, only a common desire to retreat from each other, only a common impulse to meet disagreement with force. We must admit the vanity of our false distinctions among men and learn to find our own advancement in the search for the advancement of others. We must admit in ourselves that our own children's future cannot be built on the misfortunes of others. We must recognize that this short life can neither be ennobled or enriched by hatred or revenge. Our lives on this planet are too short and the work to be done too great to let this spirit flourish any longer in our land.

Of course we cannot vanquish it with a program, nor with a solution.

But we can perhaps remember, if only for a time, that those who live with us are our brothers, that they share with us the same short moment of life; that they seek, as do we, nothing but the chance to live out their lives in purpose and in happiness, winning what satisfaction and fulfillment they can. ⌒‿

A Hope for
the Future

CHANGE AND RENEWAL

The new circumstances under which we are placed call for new words, new phrases, and for the transfer of old words to new objects. — THOMAS JEFFERSON

Men without hope, resigned to despair and oppression, do not make revolutions. It is when expectation replaces submission, when despair is touched with the awareness of possibility, that the forces of human desire and the passion for justice are unloosed.

Goethe tells us in his greatest poem that Faust lost the liberty of his soul when he said to the passing moment, "Stay, thou art so fair."

Our choice is not whether change will come, but whether we can guide that change in the service of our ideals and toward a social order shaped to the needs of all our people. In the long run we can master change not through force or fear, but only through the free work of an understanding mind, through an openness to new knowledge and fresh outlooks which can only strengthen the most fragile and the most powerful [of] human gifts: the gift of reason.

We have come out of the time when obedience, the acceptance of discipline, intelligent courage, and resolution were most important, into that more difficult time when it is a man's duty to understand his world rather than simply fight for it.

— ERNEST HEMINGWAY

A revolution is coming—a revolution which will be peaceful if we are wise enough; compassionate if we care enough; successful if we are fortunate enough—but a revolution which is coming whether we will it or not. We can affect its character; we cannot alter its inevitability.

We should, I believe, beware of the pitfalls described by Taine: "Imagine a man who sets out on a voyage equipped with a pair of spectacles that magnify things to an extraordinary degree. A hair on his hand, a spot on the tablecloth, the shifting fold of a coat, all will attract his attention; at this rate, he will not go far, he will spend his day taking six steps and will never get out of his room."

We have to get out of the room.

COMMUNITY

Together, we can make this a nation where young people do not seek the false peace of drugs. Together, we can make this a nation where old people are not shunted off; where, regardless of the color of his skin or the place of birth of his father, every citizen will have an equal chance at dignity and decency. Together, Americans are the most decent, generous, and compassionate people in the world.

Divided, they are collections of islands. Islands of blacks afraid of islands of whites. Islands of Northerners bitterly opposed to islands of Southerners. Islands of workers warring with islands of businessmen.

It is not more bigness that should be our goal. We must attempt, rather, to bring people back to . . . the warmth of community, to the worth of individual effort and responsibility... and of individuals working together as a community, to better their lives and their children's future.

An Essential Foundation

Community demands a place where people can see and know each other, where children can play and adults work together and join in the pleasures and responsibilities of the place where they live.

Action on any one front alone will not succeed. Providing a man a job, while in my judgment the most important step we can take, will not improve the schools his children attend or assure that medical care will be available even though he can afford it. Building new housing without providing social services or transportation to get to work or accessible health services will result in one slum replacing another. Improving the quality of education or job training without any promise of a job at the end will not ease the dropout rate. But action on all these matters in concert will build a community.

The city is . . . a place where men should be able to live in dignity and security and harmony, where the great achievements of modern civilization and the ageless pleasures afforded by natural beauty should be available to all.

[Another great task] is to confront the poverty of satisfaction—a lack of purpose and dignity—that inflicts us all. Too much and too long, we seem to have surrendered community excellence and community values in the mere accumulation of material things.

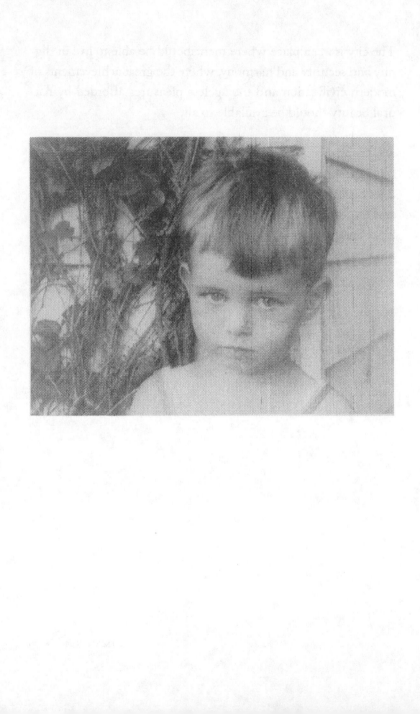

YOUTH

Your old men shall dream dreams, your young men shall see visions. And where there is no vision, life shall perish from the earth.

— SCRIPTURES

Your generation—South and North, white and blacks—[is] the first with the chance not only to remedy the mistakes which all of us have made in the past, but to transcend them. Your generation—this generation—cannot afford to waste its substance and its hope in the struggles of the past, for beyond these walls is a world to be helped, and improved, and made safe for the welfare of mankind.

The destiny of any nation, at any given time, depends on the opinions of its young men, under twenty-five.

— GOETHE

We recognize also that many young offenders may be redirected toward constructive activities through successful treatment efforts. However, these programs deal with the end results of delinquency—not the sources. We must broaden our attack and focus as much energy in the future on prevention as we have on control and treatment in the past.

This world demands the qualities of youth: not a time of life but a state of mind, a temper of the will, a quality of the imagination, a predominance of courage over timidity, of the appetite for adventure over the love of ease. It is a revolutionary world we live in, and thus, as I have said in Latin America and in Asia, in Europe and in the United States, it is young people who must take the lead.

And thus, the black American youth is powerless to change his place or to make a better one for his children. He is denied the most fundamental of human needs: the need for identity, for recognition as a citizen and as a man. Here, and not in the pitiful charade of revolutionary oratory, is the breeding ground of reverse racism, and of aimless hostility and of violence. The violent youth of the ghetto is not simply protesting his condition but making a destructive and self-defeating attempt to assert his worth and dignity as a human being, to tell us that though we may scorn his contribution, we must still respect his power.

It is your job, the task of the young people of this world, to strip the last remnants of that ancient, cruel belief [of racism and hatred] from the civilization of man.

Each nation has different obstacles and different goals, shaped by the vagaries of history and of experience. Yet as I talk to young people around the world I am impressed not by the diversity but by the closeness of their goals, their desires, and their concerns, and their hope for the future. There is discrimination in New York, the racial inequality of apartheid in South Africa, and serfdom in the mountains of Peru. People starve in the streets of India, a former Prime Minister is summarily executed in the Congo, intellectuals go to jail in Russia, and thousands are slaughtered in Indonesia; wealth is lavished on armaments everywhere in the world. These are differing evils; but they are the common works of man. They reflect the imperfections of human justice, the inadequacy of human compassion, the defectiveness of our sensibility toward the sufferings of our fellows; they mark the limit of our ability to use knowledge for the well-being of our fellow human beings throughout the world. And therefore they call upon common qualities of conscience and indignation, a shared determination to wipe away the unnecessary sufferings of our fellow human beings at home and around the world.

It is these qualities which make of youth today the only true international community.

Our answer is the world's hope; it is to rely on youth. The cruelties and obstacles of this swiftly changing planet will not yield to obsolete dogmas and outworn slogans. It cannot be moved by those who cling to a present which is already dying, who prefer the illusion of security to the excitement and danger which comes with even the most peaceful progress.

As Erik Erikson tells us, the archetype of human progress is in the story of Moses, who brought his people within sight of the promised land and then died, leaving to Joshua the leadership in achieving goals that both completely shared.

When I go down and see
the way some people live,
and look around dismayed,
shame scorches my cheeks
like the back of a flatiron.

How shamefully we hold our tongues,
or, at the most, we hem and haw . . .
Lies are written on fat faces
that should be hidden in trousers . . .

> —ANDREI VOZNESENSKY
> on the ideals "of a world of poverty
> and official lies" which RFK wrote
> "sounds remarkably like voices
> [of youth] in America."

Moreover, the youth of other nations can still see their task as the work of economic development: whether by revolutionary internal change, or by ending the economic domination—even if fancied—of the West. But the American youth, like the American nation, already knows an affluence far beyond the distant dreams of others. He only does not know what it is for.

Ah, what shall I be at fifty,
should nature keep me alive,
if I find the world so bitter
when I am but twenty-five?

— ALFRED, LORD TENNYSON

Personal Knowledge

EDUCATION

A human being is not, in any proper sense, a human being till he is educated.　　　　　　　　　　— HORACE MANN

Change is chance, which favors the mind that is prepared.

— LOUIS PASTEUR

A democratic form of government, a democratic way of life, presupposes free public education over a long period; it presupposes also an education for personal responsibility that too often is neglected.　　　　　　　　— ELEANOR ROOSEVELT

All things are at odds when God sets a thinker loose on the planet.　　　　　　　　　　　　— EDITH HAMILTON

For perhaps the greatest barrier to education in Harlem is simply a lack of hope, a lack of belief that education is meaningful to a Negro in the city of New York.

Safeguarding Civilization

Civilization is a race between education and catastrophe.

— H. G. WELLS

It is not enough that you should understand about applied science in order that your work may increase man's blessings.... Concern for man himself and his fate must always form the chief interest of all technical endeavors, concern for the great unsolved problems of the organization of labor and the distribution of goods—in order that the creations of our mind shall be a blessing and not a curse to mankind. Never forget this in the midst of your diagrams and equations.

— ALBERT EINSTEIN

We have treasured our educational system also as a firm pillar of the liberal community. This faith, however, is not unanimously shared. One critic has said: "Education [is] by its very nature an individual matter . . . not geared to mass production. It does not produce people who instinctively go the same way . . . [yet] our millions learn the same lessons and spend hours before television sets looking at exactly the same thing at exactly the same time. For one reason and another we are more and more ignoring differences, if not trying to obliterate them. We seem headed toward a standardization of the mind, what Goethe called 'the deadly commonplace that fetters us all.'" This speaker was not part of a Berkeley rally; it was Edith Hamilton, one of our greatest classicists.

The suppression of individuality—the sense that one is listening—is even more pronounced in our politics. Television, newspapers, magazines, are a cascade of words, official statements, policies, explanations, and declarations. All flow from the height of government down to the passive citizen: Who can shout up against a waterfall? More important, the language of politics is too often insincerity, which we have perhaps too easily accepted but which to the young is particularly offensive. George Orwell wrote a generation ago: "In our time, political speech and writing are largely the defense of the indefensible. Things like the continuation of British rule in India, the Russian purges and deportations, the dropping of the atom bombs on Japan, can indeed be defended, but only by arguments which are too brutal for most people to face, and which do not square with the professed aims of political parties. Thus political language has to consist largely of euphemism, question begging, and sheer cloudy vagueness. Defenseless villages are bombarded from the air, the inhabitants driven out into the countryside, the cattle machine-gunned, the huts set on fire with incendiary bullets: This is called *pacification*. Millions of peasants are robbed of their farms and sent trudging along the roads with no more than they can carry: This is called *transfer of population* or *rectification of frontiers*. People are imprisoned for years without trial, or shot in the back of the neck or sent to die of scurvy in Arctic lumber camps: This is called *elimination of unreliable elements.* The inflated style is itself a kind of euphemism. A mass of Latin words falls upon the facts like soft snow, blurring the outlines and covering up all the details." In this respect, politics has not changed since Orwell wrote. And if we add to the insincerity, and the absence of dialogue, the absurdity of a politics in which elected officials find sport in joking about children bitten by rats, we can understand why so many of our young people have turned from engagement to disengagement, from politics to passivity, from hope to nihilism, from SDS to LSD. ⌒

HISTORY

Thucydides wrote at the end of the Peloponnesian War and the end of the great age of Athens: "The kind of events that once took place will by reason of human nature take place again."

The time for extracting a lesson from history is ever at hand for those who are wise.   — DEMOSTHENES

That is the supreme value of history. The study of it is the best guaranty against repeating it.

— JOHN BUCHAN, LORD TWEEDSMUIR

To be ignorant of the past is to remain as a child.   — CICERO

Thucydides reported that the Peloponnesians and their allies were mighty in battle but handicapped by their policy-making body, in which, he related, "each presses its own ends . . . which generally results in no action at all . . . they devote more time to the prosecution of their own purposes than to the consideration of the general welfare—each supposes that no harm will come of his own neglect, that it is the business of another to do this or that; and so, as each separately entertains the same illusion, the common cause imperceptibly decays."

History is a relentless master. It has no present, only the past rushing into the future. To try to hold fast is to be swept aside.

Few will have the greatness to bend history itself; but each of us can work to change a small portion of events, and in the total of all those acts will be written the history of this generation.

TOWARD UNDERSTANDING

Nothing which does not make a man worse can harm him.

—SOCRATES

Yes, there was the sun and poverty. Then sports, from which I learned all I know about ethics. Next the war and the Resistance. And, as a result, the temptation of hatred.

—ALBERT CAMUS

"If men do not build," asks the poet, "how shall they live?"

To everything there is a season, and a time to every purpose under the heaven.

—SONG OF SOLOMON

Tragedy is a tool for the living to gain wisdom, not a guide by which we live. — WILLIAM APPLEMAN WILLIAMS

The enemies of [achieving equality] are not the black man or the white man. The enemies are fear and indifference. They are hatred and, above all, letting momentary passion blind us to a clear and reasoned understanding of the realities of our land.

Knowing that you are going to die is nothing.

— ALBERT CAMUS

No man in the whole world is free. Not one.
Slaves all to what they own or want or fear.

— UNIDENTIFIED

"The true nature of anything," Aristotle says, "is what it becomes at its highest." Not the embryo, but the full-grown man; not any man, but man at his greatest.

— EDITH HAMILTON

Saint Paul knew well that love is indissolubly joined to pain: "Love beareth all things, believeth all things, and hopeth all things." — EDITH HAMILTON

Good judgment is usually the result of experience. And experience is frequently the result of bad judgment.

There are three things which are real:
God, human folly, and laughter.
The first two are beyond our comprehension
so we must do what we can with the third.

— THE RAMAYANA

A Citizen in
a Civil Society

GOVERNMENT

Governments can err, presidents do make mistakes, but the immortal Dante tells us that Divine Justice weighs the sins of the cold-blooded and the sins of the warmhearted in a different scale. Better the occasional faults of a government living in the spirit of charity than the consistent omissions of a government frozen in the ice of its own indifference.

The Executive must be held in check; the popular branch of the Legislature strengthened, the Judiciary curbed, and the general powers of government strictly construed; but, above all, the States must be supported in exercising all their reserved rights, because, in the last resort, the States alone could make head against a central sovereign at Washington.

— HENRY ADAMS

Government is a very rough business, you must be content with very unsatisfactory results. —SIR GEORGE CORNEWALL

The inheritance of the New Deal is fulfilled. There is not a problem for which there is not a program. There is not a problem for which money is not being spent. There is not a problem or a program on which dozens or hundreds or thousands of bureaucrats are not earnestly at work.

But does this represent a solution to our problems?

Manifestly it does not.

The third element of the new politics is to halt and reverse the growing accumulation of power and authority in the central government in Washington, and to return that power of decision to the American people in their own local communities. For the truth is that with all the good that has been accomplished over the last thirty years—by unemployment compensation, Medicare, and fair labor standards; by the programs for education, housing, and community development—for all that, still the truth is that too often the programs have been close to failures.

LAW AND JUSTICE

He [President John F. Kennedy] then went on to point out that "law is the strongest link between man and freedom."

I wonder in how many countries of the world people think of law as the "link between man and freedom." We know that in many, law is the instrument of tyranny, and people think of law as little more than the will of the state, or the party—not of the people.

In a democratic society law is the form which free men give to justice. The glory of justice and the majesty of law are created not just by the Constitution—nor by the courts—nor by the officers of the law—nor by the lawyers—but by the men and women who constitute our society—who are the protectors of the law as they are themselves protected by the law.

In the state of nature, indeed, all men are born equal, but they cannot continue in this equality. Society makes them lose it, and they recover it only by the protection of the laws.

— MONTESQUIEU

Laws should be adapted to those who have the heaviest stake in the country, for whom misgovernment means not mortified pride or stinted luxuries but want and pain, and degradation and risk to their own lives and to their children's souls.

— LORD ACTON

If an obscure Florida convict named Clarence Earl Gideon had not sat down in his prison cell with a pencil and paper to write a letter to the Supreme Court, and if the Court had not taken the trouble to look for merit in that one crude petition, among all the bundles of mail it must receive every day, the vast machinery of American Law would have gone on functioning undisturbed.

Yet that we may not appear to be defective even in earthly honors, let a day be solemnly set apart for proclaiming The Charter; let it be brought forth, placed on the Divine Law, the Word of God; let a crown be placed thereon, by which the world may know, that so far as we approve of monarchy, that in America the law is king.   — THOMAS PAINE

Our long-term objective obviously is to create an international system of law and order—to create a peaceful and productive society throughout the world. We are not going to succeed this year or next, and perhaps not for many years to come. But struggle we shall and succeed we must!

As I have already told you, if at times we seemed to prefer justice to our country, this is because we simply wanted to love our country in justice, as we wanted to love her in truth and in hope.
— ALBERT CAMUS

Just saying "Obey the law" is not going to work. The law to us is a friend which preserves our property and our personal safety. But for the Negro, law means something different. Law for the Negro in the South has meant beatings and degradation and official discrimination; law has been his oppressor and his enemy.

A day or two before his death, when a rich man who knew he could bribe the jailers and get Socrates away came to him begging, "Let us save you, Socrates, your friends beseech you," Socrates said, "Dear Crito, a voice within me is telling me that I must not disobey my country's laws and do what is wrong in order to save my life."

[A judge had refused to grant bail to Dr. Martin Luther King. RFK at first agreed that his campaign should have no further involvement, but then thought more and more about the state court's action. Without telling anyone on the campaign, RFK called the judge.]
"It just burned me all the way up here on the plane. It grilled me. The more I thought about the injustice of it, the more I thought what a son of a bitch that judge was. I made it clear to him that it was not a political call; that I am a lawyer, one who believes in the right of all defendants misused in various ways . . . and I wanted to make it clear that I opposed this. I felt it was disgraceful." *[The next day King was released.]*

The Golden Rule is not sentimentality but the deepest practical wisdom. For the teaching of our time is that cruelty is contagious, and its disease knows no bounds of race or nation. Where men can be deprived because their skin is black, in the fullness of time others will be deprived because their skin is white.

To justify himself, each relies on the other's crime.

— ALBERT CAMUS

The Law and Lawyers

My dear Paul,

No one can be a truly competent lawyer unless he is a culti-vated man. If I were you, I would forget all about any technical preparation for the law. The best way to prepare for the law is to come to the study of the law as a well-read person. Thus alone can one acquire the capacity to use the English language on paper and in speech and with the habits of clear thinking which only a truly liberal education can give. No less important for a lawyer is the cultivation of the imaginative faculties by reading poetry, seeing great paintings, in the original, or in eas-ily available reproductions, and listening to great music. Stock your mind with the deposit of much good reading, and widen and deepen your feelings by experiencing vicariously as much as possible the wonderful mysteries of the universe, and forget all about your future career.

With good wishes,

Sincerely yours,

Felix Frankfurter

[During a Senate hearing]

MR. KENNEDY: Do you feel that if you gave a truthful answer to this Committee on your taking of $320,000 of Union funds that that might tend to incriminate you?

MR. BECK: It might.

MR. KENNEDY: Is that right?

MR. BECK: It might.

MR. KENNEDY: You feel that yourself?

MR. BECK: It might.

MR. KENNEDY: I feel the same way.

CHAIRMAN: We will have order, please.

How many times I have laughed at your telling me plainly that I was too lazy to be anything but a lawyer.

— ABRAHAM LINCOLN

At a Senate investigating session the man who was to be questioned took the oath and sat down, and the chairman asked, "Have you a lawyer?" The witness declared, "No, sir. I decided to tell the truth."

LEADERSHIP AND
PUBLIC SERVICE

"Some people," he said, "see things and say, 'Why?' But I dream things that never were, and I say, 'Why not?'"

— GEORGE BERNARD SHAW

[RFK often finished his stump speech with these words, and the reporters who followed the campaign used it as their cue to head back to their buses. Once, he changed the ending to "I say, 'Run for the bus.'"]

We cannot yield to the temptation to let someone else perform the job, or to remain aloof from what in a free society is everyone's business.

As for me—I welcome the challenge and the opportunity and I pledge my best effort. As Abraham Lincoln said early in the Civil War: "I do the very best I know how—the very best I can—and I mean to keep doing it so until the end. If the end brings me out all right, what is said against me won't amount to anything. If the end brings me out wrong, ten angels swearing I was right would make no difference."

The task of leadership, the first task of concerned people, is not to condemn or castigate or deplore; it is to search out the reason for disillusionment and alienation, the rationale of protest and dissent—perhaps, indeed, to learn from it. And we may find that we learn most of all from those political and social dissenters whose differences with us are most grave; for among the young, as among adults, the sharpest criticism often goes hand in hand with the deepest idealism and love of country.

I do not promise you ease. I do not promise you comfort. But I do promise you these: hardship, weariness, and suffering. And with them, I promise you victory.　　　　　—GARIBALDI

But if there was one thing President Kennedy stood for that touched the most profound feelings of young people around the world, it was the belief that idealism, high aspirations, and deep convictions are not incompatible with the most practical and efficient of programs—that there is no basic inconsistency between ideals and realistic possibilities, no separation between the deepest desires of heart and of mind and the rational application of human effort to human problems.

The Missile Crisis

[During the Cuban Missile Crisis, RFK scribbled this note on yellow legal paper and passed it to the President, during discussion of plans for the U.S. surprise air attack on Cuba.]
I now know how Tojo felt when he was planning Pearl Harbor.

At first, there was almost unanimous agreement that we had to attack early the next morning with bombers and fighters and destroy the SAM sites. But . . . the President pulled everyone back. "It isn't the first step that concerns me," he said, "but both sides escalating to the fourth and fifth step—and we don't go to the sixth because there is no one around to do so."

And so we argued and so we disagreed—all dedicated, intelligent men, disagreeing and fighting about the future of their country, and of mankind. Meanwhile, time was slowly running out.

The Russian ships were proceeding, they were nearing the five-hundred-mile barrier, and we either had to intercept them or announce we were withdrawing. I sat across the table from the President.

The thought that disturbed him the most, and that made the prospect of war much more fearful than it would otherwise have been, was the specter of the death of the children of this country and all the world—the young people who had no role, who had no say, who knew nothing even of the confrontation, but whose lives would be snuffed out like everyone else's. They would never have a chance to make a decision, to vote in an election, to run for office, to lead a revolution, to determine their own destinies.

I think these few minutes were the time of gravest concern for the President. Was the world on the brink of a holocaust? Was it our error? A mistake? Was there something further that should have been done? Or not done? For a few fleeting seconds, it was almost as though no one else was there and he was no longer the President.

At the outbreak of the First World War the ex-chancellor of Germany Prince von Bülow said to his successor, "How did it all happen?" "Ah, if only we knew," was the reply.

This was the moment we had prepared for, which we hoped would never come. The danger and concern that we all felt hung like a cloud over us all . . . These few minutes were the time of greatest worry by the President. His hand went up to his face & covered his mouth and he closed his fist. His eyes were tense, almost gray, and we just stared at each other across the table. Was the world on the bring of a holocaust and had we done something wrong? Isn't there some way we can avoid having our first exchange be with a Russian submarine—almost anything but that, he said. . . . We had come to the edge of the final decision—& the President agreed. I felt we were on the edge of a precipice and it was as if there were no way off.

I know there is a God and that He hates injustice. I see the storm coming and I see His hand in it. If He has a place and part for me, I am ready.   — ABRAHAM LINCOLN

This is a great nation and a strong people. Any who seek to comfort rather than to speak plainly, reassure rather than instruct, promise satisfaction rather than reveal frustration—they deny that greatness and drain that strength. For today as it was in the beginning, it is the truth that makes us free.

Let him who elevates himself above humanity, above its weaknesses, its infirmities, its wants, its necessities, say, if he pleases, he will never compromise; but let no one who is not above the frailties of our common nature disdain compromises.

— HENRY CLAY

History is full of peoples who have discovered it is easier to fight than think, easier to have enemies and friends selected by authority than to make their own painful choices, easier to follow blindly than to lead, even if that leadership must be the private choice of a single man alone with a free and skeptical mind. But in the final telling it is that leadership, the impregnable skepticism of the free spirit, untouchable by guns or police, which feeds the whirlwind of change and hope and progress in every land and time.

"There is," said an Italian philosopher, "nothing more difficult to take in hand, more perilous to conduct, or more uncertain in its success than to take the lead in the introduction of a new order of things."

A Share in Public Matters

There is a compelling need for a reevaluation of our public attitudes toward political life. The national attitude that politics is somehow a degrading occupation to which no man of intelligence or ambition should aspire is becoming too deeply ingrained in our national thinking.

We differ from other states in that we regard the individual who holds himself aloof from public affairs as being useless. Yet we yield to no one in our independence of spirit and complete self-reliance.   — PERICLES

Our word *idiot* comes from the Greek name for the man who took no share in public matters.   — EDITH HAMILTON

But the time is important for us to rise in defense of politics. There is no greater need than for educated men and women to point their careers toward public service as the finest and most rewarding type of life.

Politics

All the phrases which have meant so much to Americans— *peace* and *progress, justice* and *compassion, leadership* and *ideal- ism*—often sound not like stirring reminders of our nation, but call forth the cynical laughter or hostility of our young and many of our adults. Not because they do not believe them, but because they do not think our leaders mean them. . . .

This is not simply the result of bad policies and lack of skill. It flows from the fact that for almost the first time the national leadership is calling upon the darker impulses of the American spirit—not, perhaps, deliberately, but through its action and the example it sets—an example where *integrity, truth, honor,* and all the rest seem like words to fill out speeches rather than guiding beliefs. Thus we are turned inward. People wish to protect what they have. There is a failing of generosity and compassion. There is an unwillingness to sacrifice or take risks. All of this is contrary to the deepest and most dominant impulses of the American character—all that which has characterized two centuries of history.

The issue in this election, therefore, is whether this new and startling path shall continue into the future, or whether we shall turn back to our roots and to our tradition, so that future historians shall view this period as the great aberration of American history.

Politics is the pursuit of the possible, not of the ideal.

— HERBERT AGAR

[When, during the 1968 campaign, RFK's staff drew up a "maximum" civil rights platform, designed primarily for negotiating purposes, RFK adopted it fully.]
Those of you who are dealing with Southern delegations make it absolutely clear how we stand on civil rights. Don't fuzz it up. Tell the Southern states that we hope they will see other reasons why we are united as Democrats and why they should support Kennedy, but don't let there be doubt anywhere as to how the Kennedy people stand on this.

Politicians

People are just sick of politicians. And they are looking . . . for just an honest man.

There go the people—I must hurry and catch up with them, for I am their leader.

Let him say not one single word about his principles, or his creed—let him say nothing—promise nothing. Let no Committee, no convention—no town meeting ever extract from him a single word, about what he thinks now, or what he will do hereafter. Let the use of pen and ink be wholly forbidden as if he were a mad poet in Bedlam.

— NICOLAS BIDDLE,
instructions for the
campaign to nominate
William Henry Harrison
for president in 1835

To say that the future will be different from the present is, to scientists, hopelessly self-evident. I observe regretfully that in politics, however, it can be heresy. It can be denounced as radicalism or branded as subversion. There are people in every time and every land who want to stop history in its tracks. They fear the future, mistrust the present, and invoke the security of a comfortable past which, in fact, never existed.

The Life of
the Heart

The greatest of all warriors in the siege of Troy had not the pre-eminence because nature had given him strength and he carried the largest bow, but because self-discipline had taught him how to bend it. — DANIEL WEBSTER

[At the Democratic Convention in 1964, RFK thanked young people for their support of President John F. Kennedy's efforts:]
When there were difficulties, you sustained him.
When there were periods of crisis, you stood beside him.
When there were periods of happiness, you laughed with him.
And when there were periods of sorrow, you comforted him.

COURAGE

When your children and grandchildren take their place in America—going to high school, and college, and taking good jobs at good pay—when you look at them, you will say, "I did this. I was there, at the point of difficulty and danger." And though you may be old and bent from many years of labor, no man will stand taller than you when you say, "I marched with Cesar."

It is from numberless diverse acts of courage and belief that human history is shaped. Each time a man stands up for an ideal, or acts to improve the lot of others, or strikes out against injustice, he sends forth a tiny ripple of hope; and crossing each other from a million different centers of energy and daring, those ripples build a current which can sweep down the mightiest walls of oppression and resistance.

Aristotle tells us that "At the Olympic games it is not the finest and the strongest men who are crowned, but they who enter the lists. . . . So, too, in the life of the honorable and the good it is they who act rightly who win the prize." I believe that in this generation those with the courage to enter the moral conflict will find themselves with companions in every corner of the world.

He tells himself over and over again in any choice presented to him, "Prefer the hard." This holds good not only in great matters, but also in very small, in fighting by the frozen Danube and in starting the day early. — MARCUS AURELIUS

We are faced with evil. I feel rather like Augustine did before becoming a Christian when he said, "I tried to find the source of evil and I got nowhere. But it is also true that I and a few others knew what must be done if not to reduce evil at least not to add to it." Perhaps we cannot prevent this world from being a world in which children are tortured. But we can reduce the number of tortured children. And if you believers don't help us, who else in the world can help us do this? — ALBERT CAMUS

Life for him was an adventure, perilous indeed, but men are not made for safe havens. — EDITH HAMILTON

Nothing is to be feared except fear itself.

— FRANCIS BACON

We also know that only those who dare to fail greatly can ever achieve greatly.

As they waited for the attack which they knew would be the last, one of them said he had heard the Persians were so numerous that when they shot their arrows they hid the sky. "Good," said another. "Then we will fight in the shade."

— HERODOTUS

Have faith and pursue an unknown end.

— FRANCIS BACON

Few men are willing to brave the disapproval of their fellows, the censure of their colleagues, the wrath of their society. Moral courage is a rarer commodity than bravery in battle or great intelligence. Yet it is the one essential, vital quality of those who seek to change a world which yields most painfully to change.

If people bring so much courage to this world the world has to kill them or break them, so of course it kills them. The world breaks everyone, and afterward many are strong at the broken places. But those that will not break, it kills. It kills the very good and the very gentle and the very brave impartially. If you are none of those you can be sure it will kill you too, but there will be no special hurry. —ERNEST HEMINGWAY

FAMILY AND FRIENDS

I was the seventh of nine children, and when you come from that far down you have to struggle to survive.

Say hello to all the Irish Catholics for me, and tell 'em that next to John F. Fitzgerald and J. P. Kennedy I'm the toughest Irish-man that lives, which makes me the toughest man that lives.

THE WHITE HOUSE
Washington DC

November 24th, 1963

Dear Joe,

   You are the oldest of all male grandchildren. You have a special and particular responsibility now, which I know you will fulfill.

Remember all the things that Jack started—be kind to others that are less fortunate than we—and love our country.

Love to you
Daddy

For this the foolish over-careful fathers
Have broke their sleep with thoughts, their brains with care
Their bones with industry;
For this they have engrossed and piled up
The canker'd heaps of strange-achieved gold;
For this they have been thoughtful to invest
Their sons with arts and martial exercises. . . .
For what in me was purchased,
Falls upon thee in a more fairer sort.

—WILLIAM SHAKESPEARE

When I was young, I expected people to give me more than they could—continuous friendship, permanent emotions. Now I have learned to expect less of them than they can give—a silent companionship. And their emotions, their friendship, and noble gestures keep their full miraculous value in my eyes; wholly the fruit of grace.   —ALBERT CAMUS

[from a private memoir of Joseph P. Kennedy, Sr.]

What it really all adds up to is love—not love as it is described with such facility in popular magazines, but the kind of love that is affection and respect, order, encouragement, and support. He loved all of us—the boys in a very special way. Our awareness of this was an incalculable source of strength, and because real love is something unselfish and involves sacrifice and giving, we could not help but profit from it. His feeling for us was not of the devouring kind, as is true in the case of many strong men. He did not visualize himself as a sun around which satellites would circle, or in the role of a puppet master. He wanted us, not himself, to be the focal points.

He knew if he insisted on remaining in the center of national affairs, we would continue to be known as his children. He would be the dominating figure, the personality, the spokesman for the family. And in how many other families have the young been stultified. Again and again, young men with ability and talent have been kept from taking their places in the affairs of business or on the national stage because an older figure refused to make room and insisted on the glory and attention until the very end. He decided, I believe consciously, this would not happen in our family. The most important thing to him was the advancement of his children. His sole concern was to contribute to that advancement. After the end of World War II, he decided this aim could best be accomplished by doing what, for a strong figure, is probably the most difficult thing to do—to submerge his own personality. This is what he did. I can say that, except for his influence and encouragement, my brother Jack might not have run for the Senate in 1953, there would have been much less likelihood that he would have received the presidential nomination in 1960, I would not have become Attorney General, and my brother Teddy would not have run for the Senate in 1962.

He wanted us to be independent in the full sense of the term.

Beneath it all he has tried to engender a social conscience. There were wrongs which needed attention. There were people who were poor and who needed help; mentally ill who needed assistance. And we had a responsibility to them and to this country. Through no virtues and accomplishments of our own, we had been fortunate enough to be born in the United States under the most comfortable conditions. We, therefore, had a responsibility to others who were less well off.

His interest in life has been his children—not his business, not his accomplishments, not his friends, but his children. Any lasting contributions we might have made have been in a large part due to the effect he had on our lives.

SUFFERING AND TRAGEDY

He has lived a beautiful life
And has left a beautiful field,
He has sacrificed the hour
To give service for all time,
He has entered the company of the great
And with them he will be remembered forever.

— ANONYMOUS

The suffering of a soul that can suffer greatly—that and only
that is tragedy.   — EDITH HAMILTON

Having done what men could, they suffered what men must.
     — THUCYDIDES

Great spirits meet calamity greatly.   — AESCHYLUS

Only the base will long for length of life
that never turns another way from evil.
What joy is there in day that follows day,
now swift, now slow, and death the only goal.
I count as nothing him who feels within the glow of empty
    hopes.

                                        — SOPHOCLES

I share with you the same revulsion from evil. But I do not share
your hope, and I continue to struggle against this universe in
which children suffer and die.   — ALBERT CAMUS

Take heart. Suffering, when it climbs highest, lasts but a little time.
                                        — AESCHYLUS

Grief

[After his brother's death, RFK scrawled on a yellow sheet:]
The innocent suffer—how can that be possible and God be just.
All things are to be examined & called into question—
There are no limits set to thought.

[He also quoted these lines from Shakespeare's Romeo and Juliet:*]*
. . . when he shall die,
Take him and cut him out in little stars,
And he will make the face of heaven so fine
That all the world will be in love with night
and pay no worship to the garish sun.

Sagest in the council was he,
Kindest in the Hall;
Sure we never won a battle
—'Twas Owen won them all.
Soft as woman's was your voice, O'Neill: Bright was your eye,
Oh! why did you leave us, Owen?
Why did you die?

Your troubles are all over,
You're at rest with God on high,
But we're slaves, and we're orphans, Owen!—Why did
    you die?

We're sheep without a shepherd,
When the snow shuts out the sky—
Oh! why did you leave us, Owen?
Why did you die?

The long days store up many things nearer to grief than joy
... Death at the last, the deliverer.
Not to be born is past all prizing best.
Next best by far when one has seen the light
Is to go thither swiftly whence he came.
When youth and its light carelessness are past,
What woes are not without, what griefs within,
Envy and faction, strife and sudden death.
And last of all, old age, despised,
Infirm, unfriended.

— SOPHOCLES

God, whose law it is that he who learns must suffer. And even in our sleep pain that cannot forget falls drop by drop upon the heart, and in our own despair, against our will, comes wisdom to us by the awful grace of God.　　— AESCHYLUS

But sometimes in the middle of the night their wound would open afresh. And suddenly awakened, they would finger its painful edges, they would recover their suffering anew and with it the stricken face of their love.　　— ALBERT CAMUS

A Greater World

A SHARED WORLD

I am a citizen, not of Athens, nor of Greece, but of the whole world. The world is my parish. — SOCRATES

In the world, we are the most powerful of nations, controlling a destructive capacity we almost shrink from counting; yet our young men struggle, and many die, in a war in a small far-off country where our power often seems impotent. We seek the friendship of the good neighbor with the nations near our borders, and enter into a great Alliance against the age-old enemies of man; yet we are constantly called farther abroad, and our neighbors are strange to us when we return. The most populous nation in the world grows ever larger in our thoughts, with new power and wracking convulsions; yet we know little of it save a consciousness of rising danger. And above all loom the new weapons of war, threatening at every moment to destroy all they were designed to defend.

These subjects, too, have chosen themselves to be objects of our attention and concern; these, too, are symbols of a changing and churning world, recalling to us the words of Abraham Lincoln: "As our case is new, so must we think anew and act anew. We must disenthrall ourselves." As we move into the last third of this century—dangerous and bloody, but also liberating and exhilarating—that is our best guide to the future.

Restoring the Balance

Time after time, in these uncertain and dangerous years, we have reaped the consequences of neglect and delay, of misery and disease and hunger left too long to fester unremedied. . . . As President Kennedy said, "If we cannot help the many who are poor, we cannot save the few who are rich."

We cannot continue to deny and postpone the demands of our own people while spending billions in the name of the freedom of others. No nation can exert greater power of influence in the world than it can exercise over the streets of its own capital. A nation torn by injustice and violence, its streets patrolled by army units—if this is to be our country, we can doubt how long others will look to us for leadership, or seek our participation in their common ventures. America was a great force in the world, with immense prestige, long before we became a great military power. That power has come to us and we cannot renounce it, but neither can we afford to forget that the real constructive force in the world comes not from bombs but from imaginative ideas, warm sympathies, and a generous spirit. These are qualities that cannot be manufactured by specialists in public relations. They are the natural qualities of a people pursuing decency and human dignity in its own undertakings without arrogance of hostility or delusions of superiority toward others, a people whose ideals for others are firmly rooted in the realities of the society we have built for ourselves.

We should give no more assistance to a government against any internal threat than that government is capable of using itself, through its agencies and instruments. We can help them but we cannot again try to do their jobs for them.

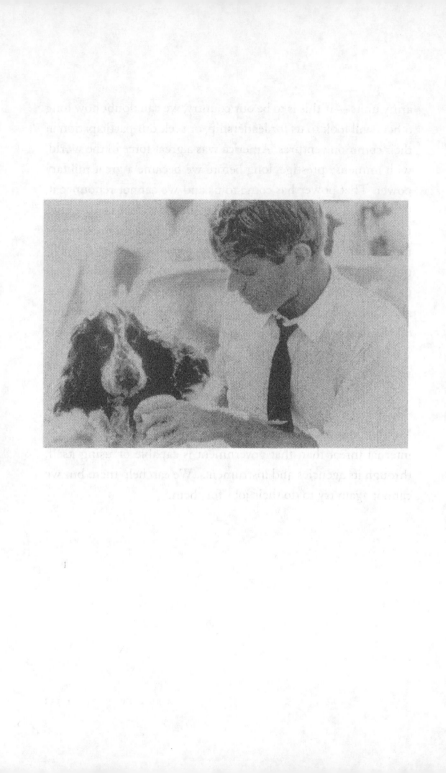

We are protected from tetanus by the work of a Japanese scientist, and from typhoid by the work of a Russian. An Austrian taught us to transfuse blood, and an Italian to protect ourselves from malaria. An Indian and the grandson of a Negro slave taught us to achieve major social change without violence.

We all owe our very existence to the knowledge and talent and effort of those who have gone before us. We have a solemn obligation to repay that debt in the coin in which it was given: to work to meet our responsibilities to that greater part of mankind which needs our assistance, to the deprived and the downtrodden, the insulted and the injured. Those men who gave us so much did not ask whether we, their heirs, would be American or South African, white or black. And we must in the same way meet our obligations to all those who need our help, whatever their nationality or the color of their skin. . . .

No longer can a spectator be certain that the blood and mud of the arena will not some day engulf him as well. No longer can any people be oblivious to the fate and future of any other. And no longer can any nation, no matter how wealthy or well-armed, be as free as it once might have been to ignore a far-off war or warning, to shrug off another nation's crisis or criticism, or to defy the concerns or the contempt of mankind. ⌒

Insurgency aims not at the conquest of territory but at the allegiance of man. That allegiance can be won only by positive programs: by land reform, by schools, by honest administration, by roads and clinics and labor unions and even-handed justice, and a share for all men in the decisions that shape their lives.

Counterinsurgency might best be described as social reform under pressure.

Any effort that disregards the base of social reform, and becomes preoccupied with gadgets and techniques and force, is doomed to failure and should not be supported by the United States.

In Africa, I tried to answer those who asked, "If the United States is fighting for self-determination in Vietnam, then how can it not support the independence struggle of Angola and Mozambique?" I answered unsatisfactorily, for there is no real answer. Yet to the questioners, it is less our intention than our pretension that is objectionable. Thus does false principle destroy the credibility of our wisdom and purpose that is the true foundation of influence as a world power.

WAR AND PEACE

Only when our arms are sufficient, without doubt, can we be certain, without doubt, that they will never have to be employed.

— JOHN F. KENNEDY

But you and I know that this war will not have any real victors and that, once it is over, we shall still have to go on living together forever on the same soil.

— ALBERT CAMUS

There is no such thing as inevitable war. If war comes it will be from failure of human wisdom.

— BONAR LAW

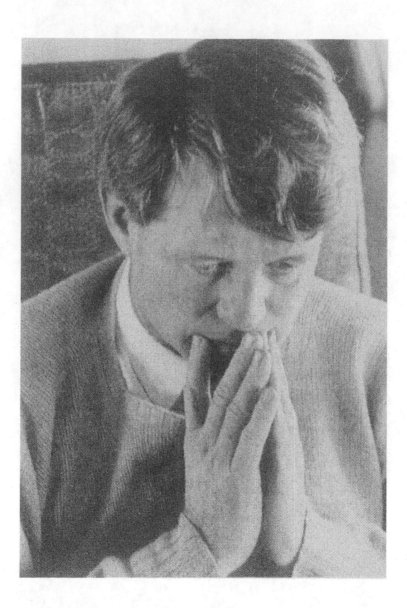

The troops will march in; the crowds will cheer; and in four days everyone will have forgotten. Then we will be told that we have to send in more troops. It is like taking a drink. The effect wears off and you have to take another.

— JOHN F. KENNEDY

It has been said that each generation must win its own struggle to be free. In our generation, thermonuclear war has made the risks of such struggles greater than ever. But the stakes are the same: the right to live in dignity according to the dictates of conscience and not according to the will of the state.

It is a great deal to fight while despising war, to accept losing everything while still preferring happiness, to face destruction while cherishing the idea of a higher civilization.

— ALBERT CAMUS

The final lesson of the Cuban missile crisis is the importance of placing ourselves in the other country's shoes.

Miscalculation and misunderstanding and escalation on one side bring a counterresponse. No action is taken against a powerful adversary in a vacuum. A government or people will fail to understand this only at their great peril. For that is how war begins—wars that no one wants, no one intends, and no one wins.

Moreover, as [Defense] Secretary [Robert] McNamara has shown, it would be in the direct self-interest of the United States and the Soviet Union to cut back our nuclear forces. For we each have more than enough to destroy the other nation, yet can never acquire enough to prevent our own destruction.

The whole question is to know whether or not we shall develop faster than the rocket with a nuclear warhead. And, unfortunately, the fruits of the spirit are slower to ripen than intercontinental missiles. But, after all, since atomic war would divest any future of its meaning, it gives us complete freedom of action. We have nothing to lose except everything. So let's go ahead. This is the wager of our generation.   —ALBERT CAMUS

We are stronger, and therefore have more responsibility, than any nation on earth; we should make the first effort—the greatest effort, and the last effort—to control nuclear weapons. We can and must begin immediately.

[RFK struggled to understand the disproportion between combat-
ants' war aims and the things done on the battlefield. Finally, the
words of Achilles in The Iliad *were most helpful to him in com-*
prehending the wrath of war:]
That makes a man go mad for all his
     goodness of reason,
that rage that rises within and swirls like
     smoke in the heart and becomes in our madness
     a thing more sweet than dripping of honey.

— HOMER

It is better to suffer certain injustices than to commit them even
to win wars, and that such deeds do us more harm than a hundred underground forces on the enemy's side.

— ALBERT CAMUS

It taught us that, contrary to what we sometimes used to think,
the spirit is of no avail against the sword, but that the spirit together with the sword will always win out over the sword alone.

— ALBERT CAMUS

[RFK visited Saigon in October 1951 with his brother, then Congressman John F. Kennedy. He wrote to his father at this time:]
Also do we stress fact that we do not care what kind of Gov [sic] a country has as long as that Gov [sic] is not controlled by a foreign nation i.e. Russia? . . . Our mistake has been not to insist on definite political reforms by the French toward the natives as prerequisites to any aid. As it stands now we are becoming more & more involved in the war to the point where we can't back out. . . . It doesn't seem to be a picture with a very bright future.

Let us reflect for a moment not on the wisdom and necessity of our cause nor on the valor of the South Vietnamese, but on the horror. For although the world's imperfections may call forth the acts of war, righteousness cannot obscure the agony and pain those acts bring to a single child.

Civilizations come and go. Great powers used to survive at the crest of their wave for several centuries. Now we will be lucky to have several generations where our power can make the difference in helping the world survive. And here we are—throwing our men, our dreams, our power into the swamps, and no one will ever understand why we did it.

If all a government can promise its people in response to insurgent activity is ten years of napalm and heavy artillery, it will not be a government for long. . . . Victory in a revolutionary war is won not by escalation but by de-escalation. . . . Air attacks by a government on its own villages are likely to be more dangerous and costly to the people than is the individual and selective terrorism of an insurgent movement.

They made a desert, and called it peace.   —TACITUS

Can we ordain to ourselves the awful majesty of God—to decide what cities and villages are to be destroyed, who will live and who will die, who will join refugees wandering in a desert of our own creation?

Whatever the costs to us, let us think of the young men we have sent there: not just the killed, but those who have to kill; not just the maimed, but also those who must look upon the results of what they do.

Thus there is another domino theory, another kind of momentum to this war. The mounting cost is an increasing deterrent to action elsewhere. Though portrayed as a necessary proof of our will and ability to "keep our commitments," the war in Vietnam is very likely to have the opposite effect. We are not only less likely to assume other commitments, but also less likely to fulfill those we have with great support or enthusiasm.

The advice "bomb them back to the Stone Age" may show that the speaker is already there himself, but it could, if followed, force all of us to join him.

To the Vietnamese, however, it must often seem the fulfillment of the prophecy of Saint John the Divine: "and I looked, and beheld a pale horse: and his name that sat on him was Death, and Hell followed with him. And power was given unto them over the fourth part of the earth, to kill with sword, with hunger, and with death."

Wise policy is a setting of priorities—differentiating between that which is merely important and that which is truly essential. And it would be both callous and self-indulgent for those of us who sit comfortably at home to form policy without full knowledge and consciousness of the costs to others, young men and women and children, whose lives turn on the abstractions of our discussion. ⌒

Epilogue

It little profits that an idle king,
by this still hearth, among these barren crags,
match'd with an aged wife, I mete and dole
unequal laws unto a savage race,
that hoard, and sleep, and feed, and know not me.
I cannot rest from travel. I will drink
life to the lees. All times I have enjoy'd
greatly, have suffer'd greatly, both with those
that loved me, and alone; on shore, and when
thro' scudding drifts the rainy Hyades
vexed the dim sea. I am become a name;
for always roaming with a hungry heart
much have I seen and known,—cities of men
and manners, climates, councils, governments,
myself not least, but honor'd of them all,—

and drunk delight of battle with my peers,
far on the ringing plains of windy Troy.
I am a part of all that I have met;
yet all experience is an arch wherethro'
gleams that untravell'd world whose margin fades
for ever and for ever when I move.
How dull it is to pause, to make an end,
to rust unburnished, not to shine in use!
As tho' to breathe were life! Life piled on life
were all too little, and of one to me
little remains: But every hour is saved
from that eternal silence, something more,
a bringer of new things; and vile it were
for some three suns to store and hoard myself,
and this gray spirit yearning in desire
to follow knowledge like a sinking star,
beyond the utmost bound of human thought.

This is my son, mine own Telemachus,
to whom I leave the sceptre and the isle,—
well-loved of me, discerning to fulfill
this labor, by slow prudence to make mild
a rugged people, and thro' soft degrees
subdue them to the useful and the good.
Most blameless is he, centred in the sphere
of common duties, decent not to fail
in offices of tenderness, and pay
meet adoration to my household gods,
when I am gone. He works his work, I mine.

There lies the port; the vessel puffs her sail;
there gloom the dark, broad seas. My mariners,
souls that have toil'd, and wrought, and thought with me,—
that ever with a frolic welcome took
the thunder and the sunshine, and opposed
free hearts, free foreheads,—you and I are old;
old age hath yet his honor and his toil;
death closes all; but something ere the end,
some work of noble note, may yet be done,
not unbecoming men that strove with Gods.
The lights begin to twinkle from the rocks;
the long day wanes; the slow moon climbs; the deep
moans round with many voices. Come, my friends.
'Tis not too late to seek a newer world.
Push off, and sitting well in order smite
the sounding furrows; for my purpose holds
to sail beyond the sunset, and the baths
of all the western stars, until I die.
I may be that the gulfs will wash us down;
it may be we shall touch the Happy Isles,
and see the great Achilles, whom we knew.
Tho' much is taken, much abides; and tho'
We are now that strength which in old days
Moved earth and heaven; that which we are, we are;
One equal temper of heroic hearts,
Made weak by time and fate, but strong in will
To strive, to seek, to find, and not to yield.

—ALFRED, LORD TENNYSON

[From Edward M. Kennedy's eulogy for RFK:]
My brother need not be idealized or enlarged in death beyond
what he was in life; rather he should be remembered simply as
a good and decent man, who saw wrong and tried to right it,
saw suffering and tried to heal it, saw war and tried to stop it.

A Brief Chronology
of RFK's Life

1925	Born November 20, Brookline, Massachusetts
1939–1942	Attended Portsmouth Priory
1942–1944	Attended Milton Academy
1944	Enrolled Harvard University; participated in Navy officer training program
1946	Seaman aboard USS *Joseph P. Kennedy, Jr.*
1948	A.B., Harvard University
1948	Visited Cairo, Israel, and Lebanon to cover Arab–Israeli conflict for the *Boston Post*
1948–1951	LL.B., University of Virginia
1950	Married Ethel Skakel
1951	Daughter Kathleen Hartington born
1951	Trip to Asia with JFK and sister Patricia
1951–1952	Attorney, Criminal Division, Department of Justice

1952	Son Joseph Patrick Kennedy II born
1952	Managed JFK's senate campaign
1952–1953	Assistant Counsel, Senate Permanent Subcommittee on Investigations (McCarthy Committee)
1953–1954	Assistant Counsel, Commission on Organization of the Executive Branch (Second Hoover Commission)
1954	Son Robert Francis, Jr., born
1954–1957	Chief Counsel to the Minority, Senate Permanent Subcommittee on Investigations
1955	Son David Anthony born
1955	Traveled to Soviet central Asia with Supreme Court Justice William O. Douglas
1956	Daughter Mary Courtney born
1957–1959	Chief Counsel, Senate Select Committee on Improper Activities in the Labor of Management Fields (McClellan Committee)
1958	Son Michael LeMoyne born
1959	Daughter Mary Kerry born
1959–1960	Managed JFK's presidential election campaign
1960	*The Enemy Within* published
1960	Appointed Attorney General of the United States
1961	Ordered U.S. marshals into Montgomery, Alabama, following attacks on Freedom Riders
1962	Goodwill tour around the world
1962	Cuban Missile Crisis

1963	Son Christopher George born
1963	JFK assassinated in Dallas, November 22
1964	Announced candidacy for U.S. Senator from New York
1964	Resigned as Attorney General
1965	Sworn in as U.S. Senator from New York
1965	Son Matthew Maxwell Taylor born
1967	*To Seek a Newer World* published
1967	Son Douglas Harriman born
1968	Announced candidacy for President of the United States
1968	Shot in the Ambassador Hotel, Los Angeles, June 5
	Died June 6
1968	Daughter Rory Elizabeth Katherine born
1969	*Thirteen Days* published

Notes

Unless otherwise indicated, all page citations (including those from press releases) refer to *RFK: Collected Speeches* (Edwin O. Guthman and C. Richard Allen, eds. New York: Viking/Penguin, 1993).

Page xix

Here in my study . . . A version of this poem was published as "For Robert Kennedy 1925–68" in Robert Lowell, *History* (New York: Farrar, Straus & Giroux, 1973).

THE ACT OF LIVING

Pages 3–7

You knew that . . . RFK, launching the Bedford-Stuyvesant restoration effort. Brooklyn, New York. December 10, 1966. Page 188.

As life is action . . . Oliver Wendell Holmes, quoted by RFK. University of Mississippi Law School Forum. Oxford, Mississippi. March 18, 1966. Page 138.

Action is with . . . Ralph Waldo Emerson, 1837. RFK's daybook (unpublished).

It is simple . . . RFK. University of Mississippi Law School Forum. Oxford, Mississippi. March 18, 1966. Page 138.

There is always . . . Daniel Webster. RFK's daybook.

God offers to . . . Ralph Waldo Emerson, "Intellect." RFK's daybook.

We all struggle . . . RFK, "A Final Message to White South Africa." University of Witwatersrand, Johannesburg, South Africa. June 8, 1966. Page 256.

He has called . . . From *The Fruitful Bough,* a privately published memoir of Joseph P. Kennedy, Sr., collected by Edward M. Kennedy. Page 210.

He only earns . . . Johann Wolfgang von Goethe. RFK's daybook.

From you. Let . . . RFK. Indiana University Medical School. April 26, 1968. Page 343.

The great French . . . RFK. National Insurance Association. Los Angeles, California. July 26, 1962. Page 88.

These were a . . . T. S. Eliot. RFK's daybook.

We are on . . . Robert Frost. RFK's daybook.

It is not . . . RFK. University of Mississippi Law School Forum. Oxford, Mississippi. March 18, 1966. Page 138.

The hottest places . . . Dante, quoted by RFK. Columbia/Barnard Democratic Club. New York, New York. October 5, 1964. Page 129.

In this theater . . . Francis Bacon, quoted by Catherine Drinker Bowen in *Francis Bacon* (New York: Fordham University Press, 1963). Page 3.

I think that . . . RFK, "Moral Implications of the War Effort." *Face the Nation.* November 26, 1967. Pages 303–4.

A journey of . . . Lao-Tzu. RFK's daybook.

AN AMERICAN SPIRIT

Pages 11–22

All of us . . . RFK. Citizens Union. New York, New York. December 14, 1967. Page 196.

History has placed . . . RFK. "National Reconciliation." University of Alabama. March 21, 1968. Page 335.

We steer our . . . Thomas Jefferson, quoted by John F. Kennedy. State of the Union address. January 14, 1963.

The essence of . . . RFK. Commencement address. Queens College. New York, New York. June 15, 1965. Page 133.

We must consider . . . RFK, "Racial Problems in the North." National Council of Christians and Jews. Chicago, Illinois. April 28, 1965. Page 158.

Think how our . . . RFK, "The Goals of American Foreign Policy." Columbus Day Dinner. Waldorf-Astoria Hotel. New York, New York. October 11, 1966. Page 262.

On this generation . . . RFK. Law Day. University of Georgia Law School. Athens, Georgia. May 6, 1961. Page 53.

But all our great . . . RFK, *To Seek a Newer World* (Garden City, N.J.: Doubleday, 1967). Pages 61–62.

Each of our . . . RFK. Subcommittee on Executive Reorganization. Washington, D.C. August 15, 1996. Page 177.

Not a decade . . . RFK. Nihon University. Tokyo, Japan. February 6, 1962. Page 75.

The American Journey . . . Archibald MacLeish, quoted by RFK. Economic Club of New York. New York, New York. November 13, 1961. Page 70.

America was a . . . RFK, "Conduct of American Foreign Policy." University of Indiana. April 24, 1968. Pages 378–79.

Over the years . . . RFK. California Institute of Technology. Pasadena, California. June 8, 1964. Page 112.

John Adams once . . . RFK, "Community, Compassion, and Involvement." Scottsbluff, Nebraska. April 20, 1968. Page 372.

Dangerous changes . . . RFK. American Trucking Association. Washington, D.C. October 20, 1959. Pages 37–38.

So if we . . . RFK, "The Value of Dissent." Vanderbilt University. Nashville, Tennessee. March 21, 1968. Pages 331–32.

Debate and dissent . . . *Ibid.*

Our ideal . . . RFK, speech planned for Rural Poverty Hearings. Page 204.

I love my . . . Albert Camus, *Resistance, Rebellion, and Death* (New York: Knopf, 1960). Page 4.

We must dare . . . RFK. Commencement address. Queens College. New York, New York. June 15, 1965. Page 133.

As long as . . . *Ibid.* Page 135.

With some trepidation . . . RFK, *Thirteen Days* (New York: W. W. Norton, 1969). Pages 16–17.

Our gross national . . . RFK, "Recapturing America's Moral Vision." University of Kansas. March 18, 1968. Pages 329–30.

Jefferson Davis once . . . RFK. University of Mississippi Law School Forum. Oxford, Mississippi. March 18, 1966. Page 139.

But one thing . . . Albert Camus, *Resistance, Rebellion, and Death.* Pages 133–34.

Pages 23–24

No citizen can . . . RFK. Portland City Club. Portland, Oregon. October 6, 1961. Page 63.

He only earns . . . Johann Wolfgang von Goethe. RFK's daybook.

We know that . . . RFK. Law Day. University of Georgia Law School. Athens, Georgia. May 6, 1961. Page 48.

Freedom means not . . . RFK. Nihon University. Tokyo, Japan. February 6, 1962. Page 77.

Thomas Paine once . . . RFK. University of Stellenbosch, South Africa. June 7, 1966. Page 250.

Freedom is not . . . RFK, "A Final Message to White South Africa." University of Witwatersrand, Johannesburg, South Africa. June 8, 1966. Page 255.

The contention was . . . Albert Camus, *Resistance, Rebellion, and Death.* Page 91.

Everything that makes . . . RFK, "Day of Affirmation." University of Cape Town, South Africa. June 6, 1966. Page 238.

A tyrant disturbs . . . Herodotus. RFK's daybook.

There is no . . . Euripides. RFK's daybook.

I believe in . . . Woodrow Wilson. RFK's daybook.

There are hazards . . . RFK. "Admitting the Enemy into the Political Process." Press release. February 19, 1966. Page 283.

The future does . . . RFK, University of California. Berkeley, California. October 22, 1996. Page 140.

For it is . . . *Ibid.* Page 141.

This is what . . . Albert Camus, *Resistance, Rebellion, and Death.* Page 13.

The Constitution protects . . . RFK, "On the Mindless Menace of Violence." Cleveland, Ohio. April 5, 1968. Page 361.

If our colleges . . . William Allen White, quoted by RFK. Kansas State University. March 18, 1968. Page 324.

Every dictatorship has . . . RFK, "The Value of Dissent." Vanderbilt University. Nashville, Tennessee. March 21, 1968. Page 332.

There are millions . . . *Ibid.*

SEEKING A BETTER WORLD

We must recognize . . . RFK, "Day of Affirmation." University of Cape Town, South Africa. June 6, 1966. Page 240.

But if any . . . RFK. University of California, Berkeley. October 22, 1966. Page 143.

They see us . . . RFK. Americans for Democratic Action. Philadelphia, Pennsylvania. February 24, 1967. Page 149.

Suppose God Is . . . RFK, "A Final Message to White South Africa." Johannesburg, South Africa. June 8, 1966. Page 257.

We live in . . . RFK, "The Conditions of Blacks in America." Michigan State University. April 11, 1968. Page 368.

But this is . . . *Ibid.* Page 369.

He is told . . . *Ibid.*

In the last . . . RFK, "The Differing Views of Racial Progress." Televised press conference. Washington, D.C. April 7, 1968. Page 363.

But as we . . . RFK, on the 1965 Watts riots. State Convention of Independent Order of Odd Fellows. Spring Valley, New York. August 18, 1965. Page 161.

It is a . . . RFK, "Solving the Urban Crisis." Subcommittee on Executive Reorganization. Washington, D.C. August 15, 1966. Page 181.

The federal government . . . RFK. Senate Commerce Committee. Washington, D.C.
July 1, 1963. Page 100.

I have bad . . . RFK, on the death of the Reverend Dr. Martin Luther King, Jr. Indianapolis, Indiana. April 4, 1968. Pages 356–57.

Among Negro youth . . . *Ibid.* Page 183.

The brutalities of . . . RFK, "Racial Problems in the North." National Council of
Christians and Jews. Chicago, Illinois. April 28, 1965. Pages 156–57.

To understand is . . . RFK, "The Conditions of Blacks in America." Michigan State
University. April 11, 1968. Page 368.

Pages 45–49

This is a . . . RFK, "On the Mindless Menace of Violence." Cleveland, Ohio. April 5,
1968. Pages 359–60.

The real threat . . . RFK, "Crime in America." Indianapolis, Indiana. April 26, 1968.
Page 381.

Thus, the fight . . . *Ibid.*

We know now . . . RFK. University of California, Berkeley. October 22, 1966. Page 144.

We have a . . . RFK, firearms legislation testimony. Washington, D.C. July 11, 1967.
Page 214.

Some look for . . . RFK, "On the Mindless Menace of Violence." Cleveland, Ohio.
April 5, 1968. Page 360.

Ninety percent of . . . RFK. Law Day. University of Georgia Law School. Athens,
Georgia. May 6, 1961. Page 48.

Among free men . . . Abraham Lincoln, quoted by RFK, "On the Mindless Menace of
Violence." Cleveland, Ohio. April 5, 1968. Page 360.

If there is . . . RFK, speech to migrant workers. Delano, California, and Monroe
County, New York. March 1966, September 1967, March 1968. Page 206.

Punishment is not . . . RFK, *To Seek a Newer World.* Page 21.

But no good . . . Albert Camus, *Resistance, Rebellion, and Death.* Page 53.

Pages 51–53

Even as the . . . RFK, "Rebuilding a Sense of Community." Worthington, Minnesota.
September 17, 1966. Page 211,

The question now . . . RFK, *To Seek a Newer World.* Pages 56–57.

One great problem . . . RFK, "Solving the Urban Crisis." Subcommittee on Executive
Reorganization. Washington, D.C. August 15, 1966. Pages 178–79.

Change is crowding . . . RFK. University of Mississippi Law School Forum. Oxford,
Mississippi. March 18, 1966. Page 136.

Therefore, the time . . . RFK, "Rebuilding a Sense of Community." Worthington, Minnesota. September 17, 1966. Page 212.

Growth has polluted . . . RFK, *To Seek a Newer World.* Page 20.

Pages 55–58

We must turn . . . RFK, "A Holiday Reflection for White America." Citizens Union. New York, New York. December 14, 1967. Page 196.

We have dealt . . . RFK, "Reforming the Welfare System." Press release. Los Angeles, California. May 19, 1968. Pages 384–85.

The jobs have . . . RFK, "A Holiday Reflection for White America." Citizens Union. New York, New York. December 14, 1967. Page 196.

In my judgment . . . RFK, *To Seek a Newer World.* Page 42.

For example, there . . . *Ibid.* Page 46.

Clearly, the most . . . RFK, "A Program for the Urban Crisis." Borough President's Conference of Community Leaders. New York, New York. January 21, 1966. Pages 169–70.

But the root . . . RFK, "Reforming the Welfare System." Press release. Los Angeles, California. May 19, 1968. Page 385.

The answer to . . . *Ibid.*

Our society—all . . . RFK, on the 1965 Watts riots. State Convention of Independent Order of Odd Fellows. Spring Valley, New York. August 18, 1965. Pages 159–60.

If I worked . . . RFK, on redirecting United States policy in Latin America. United States Senate. May 9 and 10, 1996. Page 226.

Look through the . . . RFK, "A Holiday Reflection for White America." Citizens Union. New York, New York. December 14, 1967. Page 195.

Pages 59–63

Action in adequate . . . RFK, "Child Poverty and Hunger." University of Notre Dame. South Bend, Indiana. April 4, 1968. Pages 353–54.

For there is . . . RFK, "On the Mindless Menace of Violence." Cleveland, Ohio. April 5, 1968. Page 360.

"Well, what joy . . . Sophocles, quoted by RFK. Columbia/Barnard Democratic Club. New York, New York. October 5, 1964. Page 129.

The poor man's . . . John Adams, quoted by RFK, *To Seek a Newer World.* Page 35.

Our housing projects . . . RFK, "Solving the Urban Crisis." Subcommittee on Executive Reorganization. Washington, D.C. August 15, 1966. Page 180.

Let [television] show . . . RFK, "A Holiday Reflection for White America." Citizens Union. New York, New York. December 14, 1967. Pages 193–94.

There are others . . . RFK, speech planned for Rural Poverty Hearings. Page 203.
And there are others . . . *Ibid.*

Pages 65–69

We often quote . . . RFK, "Reforming the Welfare System." Press release. Los Angeles, California. May 19, 1968. Page 385.
And the effects . . . RFK, "A Program for the Urban Crisis." Borough President's Conference of Community Leaders. New York, New York. January 21, 1966. Page 170.
If we cannot . . . RFK, "Reforming the Welfare System." Press release. Los Angeles, California. May 19, 1968. Page 385.
So there is . . . RFK, "Child Poverty and Hunger." University of Notre Dame. South Bend, Indiana. April 4, 1968. Page 353.
But of all . . . RFK, "Achieving Racial Understanding." Fort Wayne, Indiana. April 10, 1968. Page 366.
The oppressed want . . . Albert Camus, *Resistance, Rebellion, and Death.* Page 94.
We learn, at . . . RFK, "Day of Affirmation." University of Cape Town, South Africa. June 6, 1966. Page 244.

A HOPE FOR THE FUTURE

Pages 73–75

The new circumstances . . . Thomas Jefferson. RFK's daybook.
Men without hope . . . RFK. University of California, Berkeley. October 22, 1966. Page 143.
Goethe tells us . . . Johann Wolfgang von Goethe. RFK's daybook.
Our choice is . . . RFK, "A Final Message to White South Africa." University of Witwatersrand, Johannesburg, South Africa. June 8, 1966. Page 255.
We have come . . . Ernest Hemingway, 1946. RFK's daybook.
A revolution is . . . RFK, "Redirecting United States Policy in Latin America." United States Senate. Washington, D.C. May 9 and 10, 1966. Page 228.
We should, I . . . RFK. Air Pollution Control Conference. New York, New York. January 4, 1967. Page 213.

Pages 77–79

Together, we can . . . RFK, "Johnson's Appeal to the Darker Impulses of the American Spirit." Greek Theatre. Los Angeles, California. March 24, 1968, Page 337.
It is not . . . RFK, "Rebuilding a Sense of Community." Worthington, Minnesota. September 17, 1966. Page 212.

Community demands a . . . RFK, "Solving the Urban Crisis." Subcommittee on Executive Reorganization. Washington, D.C. August 15, 1966. Page 179.

Action on any . . . RFK, "Meeting the Urban Crisis." Press release. *Congressional Record.* May 31, 1968. Pages 392–93.

The city is . . . RFK, "Solving the Urban Crisis." Subcommittee on Executive Reorganization. Washington, D.C. August 15, 1966. Page 178.

[Another great task] . . . RFK, "Recapturing America's Moral Vision." University of Kansas. March 18, 1968. Page 329.

Pages 81–85

Your old men . . . Scriptures, quoted by RFK, "America's Approach to Wars of Liberation." International Police Academy. Washington, D.C. July 9, 1965. Page 279.

Your generation—South . . . RFK. University of Mississippi Law School Forum. Oxford, Mississippi. March 18, 1966. Page 136.

The destiny of . . . Johann Wolfgang von Goethe. RFK's daybook.

We recognize also . . . RFK. National Committee for Children and Youth Conference on Unemployed, Out-of-School Youth in Urban Areas. Washington, D.C. May 24, 1961. Page 59.

This world demands . . . RFK, "Day of Affirmation." University of Cape Town, South Africa. June 6, 1966. Page 243.

And thus, the . . . RFK, "The Conditions of Blacks in America." Michigan State University. April 11, 1968. Page 369.

It is your . . . RFK, "Day of Affirmation." University of Cape Town, South Africa. June 6, 1966. Page 241.

Our answer is . . . *Ibid.* Pages 242–43.

As Erik Erikson . . . RFK, *To Seek a Newer World.* Page 11.

When I go . . . *Ibid.* Page 14.

Moreover, the youth . . . *Ibid.* Page 15.

Ah, what shall . . . Alfred, Lord Tennyson, quoted by RFK, *To Seek a Newer World.* Page 17.

PERSONAL KNOWLEDGE

Pages 89–93

A human being . . . Horace Mann. RFK's daybook.

Change is chance . . . Louis Pasteur. RFK's daybook.

A democratic form . . . Eleanor Roosevelt. RFK's daybook.

All things are . . . Edith Hamilton, RFK's daybook.

For perhaps the . . . RFK, "A Program for the Urban Crisis." Borough President's
Conference of Community Leaders. New York, New York. January 21–22, 1966.
Page 170.
Civilization is a . . . H. G. Wells. RFK's daybook.
It is not . . . Albert Einstein, quoted by RFK. California Institute of Technology.
Pasadena, California. June 8, 1964. Page 111.
We have treasured . . . RFK, *To Seek a Newer World.* Pages 7–8.
The suppression of . . . Ibid. Pages 8–9.

Pages 95–96

Thucydides wrote at . . . Thucydides. RFK's daybook.
The time for . . . Demosthenes. RFK's daybook.
That is the . . . John Buchan, Lord Tweedsmuir. RFK's daybook.
To be ignorant . . . Cicero. RFK's daybook.
Thucydides reported that . . . Edith Hamilton, RFK's daybook.
History is a . . . RFK, "The Goals of American Foreign Policy." Columbus Day
Dinner. Waldorf-Astoria Hotel. New York, New York. October 11, 1966. Pages
262–63.
Few will have . . . RFK, "Day of Affirmation." University of Cape Town, South
Africa. June 6, 1966. Page 243.

Pages 97–99

Nothing which does . . . Socrates. RFK's daybook.
Yes, there was . . . Albert Camus, *Resistance, Rebellion, and Death.* Page 242.
"If men do . . . RFK, launching the Bedford-Stuyvesant restoration effort. Brooklyn,
New York. December 10, 1966. Page 186.
To everything there . . . The Song of Solomon, quoted by RFK, "A Holiday Reflec-
tion for White America." Citizens Union. New York, New York. December 14,
1967. Page 194.
Tragedy is a . . . William Appleman Williams, quoted by RFK, "Ending the War in
Vietnam." Kansas State University. March 18, 1968. Page 325.
The enemies of . . . RFK, "Achieving Racial Understanding." Fort Wayne, Indiana.
April 10, 1968. Page 367.
Knowing that you . . . Albert Camus, *Resistance, Rebellion, and Death.* Page 201.
No man in . . . Unknown speaker, quoted from Edith Hamilton, *The Echo of Greece*
(New York: W. W. Norton & Co., 1957). Page 36.
"The true nature . . . Ibid. Page 164.
Saint Paul knew . . . Ibid. Page 167.

Good judgment is . . . Unattributed quotation passed from Robert Lovett to RFK during the Cuban missile crisis. See Arthur M. Schlesinger, Jr., *Robert Kennedy and His Times* (Boston: Houghton Mifflin Company, 1978). Page 532.

There are three . . . Aubrey Menen, *The Ramayana,* inscribed by RFK on a silver beer mug. *Robert Kennedy and His Times.* Page 602.

A CITIZEN IN A CIVIL SOCIETY

Pages 103–104

Governments can err . . . Franklin Delano Roosevelt, inaugural address, January 4, 1946.

The Executive must . . . Henry Adams. RFK's daybook.

Government is a . . . Sir George Cornewall. RFK's daybook.

The inheritance of . . . RFK, "Redirecting Government, Solving Problems." Utica, New York. February 7, 1966. Pages 208–9.

The third element . . . RFK, "Forging a New Politics." San Francisco, California. May 21, 1968. Page 389.

Pages 105–111

He [President John] . . . RFK. Law Day. University of Georgia Law School. Athens, Georgia. May 6, 1961. Page 47.

In a democratic society . . . RFK, 1962. Caption under a framed photograph of RFK at his family home, Hickory Hill.

In the state . . . Montesquieu. RFK's daybook.

Laws should be . . . Lord Acton. RFK's daybook.

If an obscure . . . RFK. Senate Commerce Committee. Washington, D.C. July 1, 1963. Pages 100–1.

Yet that we . . . Thomas Paine. RFK's daybook.

Our long-term objective . . . RFK. Portland City Club. Portland, Oregon. October 6, 1961. Page 62.

As I have . . . Albert Camus, *Resistance, Rebellion, and Death.* Page 13.

Just saying "Obey . . . RFK, on the 1965 Watts riots. State Convention of Independent Order of Odd Fellows. Spring Valley, New York. August 18, 1965. Page 162.

A day or two . . . Socrates. RFK's daybook.

"It just burned . . . RFK, quoted in Arthur M. Schlesinger, Jr., *Robert Kennedy and His Times.* Pages 217–18.

The Golden Rule . . . RFK, "A Final Message to White South Africa." University of Witwatersrand, Johannesburg, South Africa. June 8, 1966. Page 255.

To justify himself . . . Albert Camus, *Resistance, Rebellion, and Death.* Page 116.

My dear Paul . . . Felix Frankfurter. RFK's daybook.

Do you feel . . . RFK, *The Enemy Within* (New York: Harper, 1960). Page 31.

How many times . . . Abraham Lincoln to Colonel E. D. Taylor. RFK's daybook.

At a Senate . . . RFK's daybook.

Pages 113–125

"Some people," he . . . George Bernard Shaw. RFK's daybook.

We cannot yield . . . RFK. Portland City Club. Portland, Oregon. October 6, 1961. Page 63.

The task of . . . RFK, *To Seek a Newer World.* Page 3.

I do not . . . Garibaldi, quoted by RFK, "The Goals of American Foreign Policy." Columbus Day Dinner. Waldorf-Astoria Hotel. New York, New York. October 11, 1966. Page 264.

But if there . . . RFK, "Day of Affirmation." University of Cape Town, South Africa. June 6, 1966. Page 244.

I now know . . . RFK, *Thirteen Days.* Page 9.

At first, there . . . *Ibid.* Page 76.

And so we . . . *Ibid.* Page 13.

The Russian ships . . . *Ibid.* Page 46.

The thought . . . *Ibid.* Page 84.

I think these . . . *Ibid.* Pages 47–48.

At the outbreak . . . *Ibid.* Page 106.

This was the . . . RFK, writing in his private papers during the height of the Cuban missile crisis. See Arthur M. Schlesinger, Jr., *Robert Kennedy and His Times.* Page 514. This passage, somewhat rewritten, also appears in RFK, *Thirteen Days.* Pages 48–49.

I know there . . . Abraham Lincoln. RFK's daybook.

This is a . . . RFK, "Illusions in the Aftermath of Tet." Chicago, Illinois. February 8, 1968. Page 311.

Let him who . . . Henry Clay. RFK's daybook.

History is full . . . RFK, "A Final Message to White South Africa." University of Witwatersrand, Johannesburg, South Africa. June 8, 1966. Page 256.

"There is," said . . . RFK, "Day of Affirmation." University of Cape Town, South Africa. June 6, 1966. Page 243.

There is a . . . RFK. American Trucking Association. Washington, D.C. October 20, 1959. Page 34.

We differ from . . . Pericles, in a funeral oration, quoted by RFK. Columbia/Barnard Democratic Club. New York, New York. October 5, 1964. Page 129.

Our word idiot . . . Edith Hamilton, *The Greek Way*. Page 225.

But the time . . . RFK. American Trucking Association. Washington, D.C. October 20, 1959. Page 34.

All the phrases . . . RFK, "Johnson's Appeal to the Darker Impulses of the American Spirit." Greek Theatre. Los Angeles, California. March 24, 1968. Page 338.

Politics is the . . . Herbert Agar. RFK's daybook.

Those of you . . . RFK. Arthur M. Schlesinger, Jr., *Robert Kennedy and His Times*. Page 215.

People are just . . . RFK, "Forging a New Politics." San Francisco, California. May 21, 1968. Page 390.

There go the . . . RFK's daybook.

Let him say . . . Nicolas Biddle. RFK's daybook. Page 47.

To say that . . . RFK. California Institute of Technology. Pasadena, California. June 8, 1964. Page 113.

THE LIFE OF THE HEART

Page 129

The greatest of . . . Daniel Webster. RFK's daybook.

When there were . . . RFK. Democratic National Convention. Atlantic City, New Jersey. August 27, 1964. Page 116.

Pages 131–135

When your children . . . RFK, speech to migrant workers. Delano, California, and Monroe County, New York. March 1966, September 1967, March 1968. Page 205.

It is from . . . RFK, "Day of Affirmation." University of Cape Town, South Africa. June 6, 1966. Pages 243–44.

Aristotle tells us . . . *Ibid*. Page 245.

He tells himself . . . Marcus Aurelius. RFK's daybook.

We are faced . . . Albert Camus. RFK's daybook.

Life for him . . . Edith Hamilton, on Aeschylus. RFK's daybook.

Nothing is to . . . Francis Bacon. RFK's daybook.

We also know . . . RFK, "Day of Affirmation." University of Cape Town, South Africa. June 6, 1966. Page 244.

As they waited . . . Herodotus, quoted by Edith Hamilton, *The Greek Way*. Page 160.

Have faith and . . . Francis Bacon. RFK's daybook.

Few men are . . . RFK, "Day of Affirmation." University of Cape Town, South Africa. June 6, 1966. Pages 244–45.

If people bring . . . Ernest Hemingway, *A Farewell to Arms* (New York: Scribner, 1929). Page 186.

Pages 137–141

I was the . . . RFK. Arthur M. Schlesinger, Jr., *Robert Kennedy and His Times.* Page 23.
Say hello to . . . *Ibid.* Page 53.
THE WHITE HOUSE . . . *Ibid.* Page 612.
For this the . . . William Shakespeare, *Henry IV,* quoted by RFK. Arthur M. Schlesinger, Jr., *Robert Kennedy and His Times.* Page 820.
When I was . . . Albert Camus. RFK's daybook.
What it really . . . From *The Fruitful Bough,* a privately published memoir of Joseph P. Kennedy, Sr., collected by Edward M. Kennedy. Pages 210–15.

Pages 143–147

He has lived . . . Unknown. Written to commemorate the death of a young soldier. 1916. RFK's daybook.
The suffering of . . . Edith Hamilton. RFK's daybook.
Having done what . . . Thucydides, on the mines in Syracuse. RFK's daybook.
Great spirits meet . . . Aeschylus. RFK's daybook.
Only the base . . . Attributed to Sophocles in RFK's daybook.
I share with . . . Albert Camus. RFK's daybook.
Take heart. Suffering . . . Aeschylus, quoted by Edith Hamilton, *The Greek Way.* Page 223.
The innocent suffer . . . RFK. Arthur M. Schlesinger, Jr., *Robert Kennedy and His Times.* Page 617.
. . . *when he shall die* . . . William Shakespeare, *Romeo and Juliet,* Act 3, Scene 2.
Sagest in the council . . . RFK, in a speech to the Friendly Sons of St. Patrick of Lackawanna County. Scranton, Pennsylvania. March 17, 1964. Page 120.
The long days . . . Sophocles. RFK's daybook.
God, whose law . . . Aeschylus. RFK's daybook.
But sometimes in . . . Albert Camus. RFK's daybook.

A GREATER WORLD

Pages 151–156

I am a . . . Socrates. RFK's daybook.
In the world . . . RFK, *To Seek a Newer World.* Page xvi.
Time after time . . . RFK, on redirecting United States policy in Latin America. United States Senate. May 9 and 10, 1966. Page 229.
We cannot continue . . . RFK, "Conduct of American Foreign Policy." University of Indiana. April 24, 1968. Pages 378–79.
We should give . . . RFK, "Conduct of American Foreign Policy." University of Indiana. April 24, 1968. Pages 376–77.

We are protected . . . RFK. University of Stellenbosch, South Africa. June 7, 1966. Pages 248–49.

Insurgency aims not . . . RFK. Arthur M. Schlesinger, Jr., *Robert Kennedy and His Times*. Page 463.

In Africa, I . . . *Ibid*. Page 164.

Pages 157–164

Only when our . . . JFK, quoted by RFK. Democratic National Convention. Atlantic City, New Jersey. August 27, 1964. Page 116.

But you and . . . Albert Camus, *Resistance, Rebellion, and Death*. Page 130.

There is no . . . Bonar Law. RFK's daybook.

The troops will . . . JFK, quoted by RFK, commenting on his press release about admitting the enemy into the political process. Page 282.

It has been said . . . RFK. Testimonial dinner for John Reynolds. Milwaukee, Wisconsin. October 6, 1962. Page 93.

It is a . . . Albert Camus, *Resistance, Rebellion, and Death*. Pages 6–7.

The final lesson . . . RFK, unfinished chapter of *Thirteen Days*. See *Collected Speeches*. Page 94.

Miscalculation . . . RFK, *Thirteen Days*. Page 103.

Moreover, as [Defense] . . . RFK, "Controlling the Spread of Nuclear Weapons." United States Senate. Washington, D.C. June 23, 1965. Page 221.

The whole question . . . Albert Camus, *Resistance, Rebellion, and Death*. Page 246.

We are stronger . . . RFK, "Controlling the Spread of Nuclear Weapons." United States Senate. Washington, D.C. June 23, 1965. Page 221.

That makes a . . . Homer, *The Iliad*, Book XVIII; quoted by RFK, *To Seek a Newer World*. Page 150.

It is better . . . Albert Camus, *Resistance, Rebellion, and Death*. Page 114.

It taught us . . . *Ibid*. Page 9.

Also do we . . . RFK. Arthur M. Schlesinger, Jr., *Robert Kennedy and His Times*. Page 92.

Let us reflect . . . RFK, "A Break with the Administration and a Plan for Peace." United States Senate. Washington, D.C. March 2, 1967. Page 293.

Civilizations come and . . . *Ibid*. Page 292.

If all a government . . . RFK, "America's Approach to Wars of Liberation." International Police Academy. Washington, D.C. July 9, 1965. Page 275.

They made a . . . RFK, "Ending the War in Vietnam." Kansas State University. March 18, 1968. Page 325.

Can we ordain . . . *Ibid*. Page 326.

Whatever the costs . . . *Ibid.*
Thus there is . . . RFK, *To Seek a Newer World.* Pages 197–98.
The advice "bomb . . . *Ibid.* Page 203.
To the Vietnamese . . . *Ibid.* Page 205.

Pages 165–168

It little profits . . . Alfred, Lord Tennyson, "Ulysses." *Tennyson's Poetry* (Robert W. Jill, Jr., ed. New York: W. W. Norton, 1971). Pages 52–54.
My brother need . . . Edward M. Kennedy, *Eulogy for Robert F. Kennedy.*

PHOTOGRAPH CREDITS